Invisible Jim Crow

Invisible
JIM CROW

Contemporary Ideological
Threats to the Internal
Security of African Americans

Michael Tillotson

AFRICA WORLD PRESS
TRENTON | LONDON | CAPE TOWN | NAIROBI | ADDIS ABABA | ASMARA | IBADAN

AFRICA WORLD PRESS
541 West Ingham Avenue | Suite B
Trenton, New Jersey 08638

Book and cover design: Saverance Publishing Services

Tillotson, Michael.
  Invisible Jim Crow : contemporary ideological threats to the internal security of African Americans / Michael Tillotson.
     p. cm.
  Includes bibliographical references and index.
  ISBN 1-59221-801-6 (cloth) -- ISBN 1-59221-802-4 (pbk.)
     1.   African Americans--Psychology. 2.   African Americans--Race identity. 3.   African Americans--Social conditions--21st century. 4. United States--Race relations--21st century. 5. United States--Social conditions--21st century. I. Title.
  E185.625.T55 2011
  305.896'073--dc22
                              2010054291

This book is dedicated to my grandfather Mr. Clyde Zellers Sr.

Table of Contents

Foreword I
BY MOLEFI KETE ASANTE

President Ronald Reagan was a pivotal American political figure. He championed the American vision of itself as the greatest country on earth and became the individual incarnation of the thrusting chests of a collective white America. While all Americans did not participate in this cowboy symbolism of one true hero against the world, most of those who accepted the Reagan doctrine also accepted his domestic stance. This was the fundamental problem with the Reagan years. There had been Vietnam and then there was Iran and the cowboy rode into town from being governor of California to rid the world of its wrongs. Reagan's entry into national politics awakened in the dominant white population a desire for revenge, a new place in the sun, hubris, and the search for old values. Michael Tillotson has written about the implications of this entire era with insight, expertise, and rationality and those of us who have had the privilege of reading his work and conversing with him know that he has begun a revolutionary appraisal of the American society.

Michael Tillotson is right to see the Republican Revolution, as it was called, and the Contract with America for what it represented to African Americans: the rise of the neoconservative political activist. Using a strong methodological framework to discuss the relationship between the neoliberals and neoconservatives Tillotson charts how their engagement was mutually beneficial to all sides. He is at once brilliant, intelligent in his judgment, and precise in his criticism.

Of course, none of this could take place without some construction of the African by a racist society. Alas, the construction is not merely one of the African as victim but as not human, not capable of the same agency that one finds in other humans, and this is the worst form of racism because this style of racism denies the humanity of Africans. In this book Tillotson challenges us to see the invisibility and otherness that constitute the pillars upon which dominative social construction is erected.

In my judgment it is not the Post-Racial Project that will win the discourse battle for attention in the next few years but the renewal of a discourse around the question of privilege, white privilege, in the era of post raciality. In other words, while the principal propaganda will be the issue of post raciality, as long as we see this as the Obama era, there will be the advancement of white privilege in reality. It is wrong to assume that society has undergone the transformation that is needed to reduce racism simply by the act of electing Barack Obama to the presidency. Perhaps we are in the strange and bizarre place where people can speak of post raciality yet operate in a most racist manner.

The courage of Tillotson to take on the misdirection, as he calls it, of the Black church, is remarkable because herein is the major contradiction of the African American population. While Tillotson is much more liberal in his appreciation and sensitivity to the church than I am, he nevertheless produces a powerful critique of the concept of the Word Church theological construction. Of course, it appears to me that the real problematic with the idea that there is a God whose requirement that humans be children of God complicates the lives of Black people who could never see themselves in the light of the God that has been created, projected, and imaged for Africans by the white ministers and missionaries. To be a child of God is to be in the image of God and the Black person is not presented as in the image of God by anyone, neither the Black adherents or white votarists of Christianity, and so, neither can really be counted on to accept the Black person as a child of God. Furthermore, the diversion to whiteness as an approach to God is an indication that the religion itself is problematic. Who is this God? Has the African in the Americas really created a God who could create them? I mean once you have created God then the God can create you because the ideas, concepts, qualifications, attributes, and desires of that God are the same ones that draw the people to the ideals of the metaphor we call God.

This is not the fundamental emphasis of Tillotson's work but his concentration on the European worldview, to be precise, is a focus on how the operational ethos of American culture has affected the lives of black people in a negative way. The argument here is that the entire European project has been articulated against the interests of African people, producing cultural dislocation, emotional immaturity, and psychological disorientation. In proposing the Doctrine of Wellness of Being, an optimum system for retrieval of culture, Tillotson seeks to refocus African Americans to original constructs, in a reclamation of values and views. There is nothing pejorative or parochial in this view, only a response to racial and cultural conditions that stifle the full development of the human personality.

One cannot take lightly this project for a new world, not a post racial world since we have been living in post raciality since the very beginning of the racial classification system, but a new world where the old hierarchies of race and rank have been degraded and cast to the side for a more robust ethic of Maat in the classical African sense of balance, order, and harmony through our common humanity. Nothing can keep me away from announcing this book as one of the best treatments of the themes of domination in contemporary times and from stating that Michael Tillotson has taken the critical baton for a new generation of scholars.

MOLEFI KETE ASANTE is Professor in the Department of African American Studies at Temple University. He has published over 70 books and written more than 400 articles and essays for journals, books and magazines and is the founder of the theory of Afrocentricity. In the fall of 1984 Dr. Asante became chair of the African American Studies Program at Temple University where he created the first Ph.D. Program in African American Studies in 1987. He has directed more than 140 Ph.D. dissertations.

Foreword II
BY LEWIS R. GORDON

> *"Said it was 96 degrees in the shade...*
> *You caught me on the loose*
> *fighting to be free*
> *now you show me a noose*
> *... real hot in the shade"*
> —Third World, "1865 (96 Degrees in the Shade)"

Michael Tillotson wrote this book as, in his words, "a mercenary of an emancipating vision for African Americans." His goal, as an intellectual, is to offer to African Americans, and by extension the African Diaspora, words of wisdom for no less than the liberation of the mind.

But the mind is not, as some would have it, an abstract, free-floating signifier. The mind is an embodied reality of flesh and blood, situated in a world of other human beings. A world of human beings is a world of needs marked not only by the classic wants of food, clothing, and shelter, but also the social demands of history, culture, and the dignity borne of agency and political life.

Liberation of the mind, then, requires ideas that affect these wider dimensions of African American cultural and political life. The intellectual's tools and weapons, however, are her or his ideas. Their purpose is to intervene and transform assaults on the spirit, forms of symbolic violence whose effects are on a continuum with the history of torture, lynching and mob violence, and state-sanctioned terrorism against the humanity of a people whose labor was the backbone of a large portion of modern wealth ranging from the material infrastructure of the modern world to many cultural and technological innovations.

Tillotson's goal is liberation itself. Such a task involves offering a different portrait of the contemporary situation of African Americans than those offered by dominant narratives. Those narratives offer a portrait of American life that is consistently noble and virtuous. It is of a nation committed to freedom and the affirmation of human rights. It is of opportunity and prosperity. When, however, African American intellectuals and other critics speak of enslavement, colonization, racism, and policies premised upon systemic poverty, the response is often to treat such intellectuals as proverbial messengers who should be killed.

The path of turning one's eyes away from the contradictions of one's society has received challenges throughout. From Lemuel Haynes in the 18th century to David Walker and Martin Delany in the 19th to W.E.B. DuBois and Anna Julia Cooper through to Malcolm X and many others in the 20th, to the critical intellectual community of which Tillotson is a member in the 21st century, the position has been resolute. A genuine struggle for freedom involves not blaming the people for their enslavement. The fight for freedom must be accompanied by a clear and accurate diagnosis of the social conditions by which enslavement was formed and persists.

A form of blaming the victims is, as DuBois argued, the construction of "problem people." This involves the rhetorical technique of making African Americans into problems instead of addressing the problems they face in an anti-Black racist society. Among the ideological features of this approach is its theodicean form. Theodicy involves the demonstration of the goodness of G-d in the face of evil and injustice. Classic theodicean arguments are twofold: (1) G-d is beyond human comprehension and (2) evil and injustice are a function of human abuse of G-d's generosity of endowing humanity with free will. In both instances, the deity is without fault and the problem of evil and injustice is blamed on human beings.

A form of idolatry has emerged in the modern world with systems taking the place of G-d in theodicean forms of rationalization. Thus, the apologists of white supremacist America treat American society as all good and its contradictions as a function of activities of people outside the system—in other words, problem people whose fault is their failure to live in the system.

What, however, if the system is designed for the failure of such people? The contradiction becomes obvious: African Americans receive double blame—for not being part of a system whose incorporation promises their dehumanization. Put differently, it is a form of damned if you do, damned if you don't thesis: to be inside is to fail; to be outside means to fail.

African Americans thus face a neurotic situation in American society, one, as Frantz Fanon has shown, African Diasporic people face in the modern world. We are asked to seek recognition in societies expecting us to leave ourselves outside as we enter. It is neurotic because it is an aim-inhibiting demand. It is a dangerous exemplar of the problem people thesis, since the logical response to problems is to get rid of them, and too many of us are aware of the trauma offered by that road.

There have been many responses to the construction of African Americans as problem people. Some have embraced the concept and encouraged African Americans to participate in our own disappearance. Learn to no longer to be black, African, or African American, they urge, and become simply and only American. There have been many critical responses to this thesis. I think the Native American philosopher Viola Cordova offers a poignant one: "The value of survival is being able to recognize yourself after you've managed to survive."

Another route is to identify the problem of being formulated as problems in the first place and devote one's energies to addressing the contradictions of the society that created them. Paraphrasing Richard Wright, there is no black problem; there is a white problem, white attitudes toward black people and the use of power to block the path of freedom.

There is, however, an African American problem worth considering, and that is the extent to which there are African Americans who have bought into the first response of seeking their own degradation and disappearance. There is also the problem of confusion, as Tillotson formulates it, of being caught in a web of self-deceiving, bad faith ideological perspectives to the point of being inactive, of being, in his words, "resistant to resistance." Tillotson's mercenary work on behalf of African Americans comes to the fore here, then, as an effort to offer the critically clear and accurate portrait of the American narrative on race needed to eliminate this confusion.

Tillotson's critique is sobering. Aside from brief respites, the American experience has been governed by a war on African people. National integrity, governed by an ideology of racial purity, called for a form of social and historical cleansing in which, consistently, African Americans have been a focus. Tillotson's critical historical study offers a genealogy of this ideology. Neoconservative ideology is one culprit in this regard and the other is neoliberalism. Together, these twins of the move from slightly left of center to the right depend on rationalizations of reality devoid of verification and rigor of analysis. Particularly with regard to race, their proponents work more through fictional and often mythic tropes than reality supported by empirical evidence. This is, for example, the case with the welfare queen figure of the Reagan era and the black criminal of the George H.W. Bush period.

The neoconservatives, whose mouthpieces include Dinesh D'Souza and John McWhorter, offer the construction of African Americans as depraved, diseased, deviant, delinquent, and intellectually deficient. The correlated disciplinary rationalizations of this ideology are black people as problems of judicial and criminal justice studies, health, and education. The specific correlates are studies of crime, AIDS, and intellectual deficiency. Their work is theodicean in the sense discussed above. The United States and the entire modern Western tradition are without fault, and the plight of the many whose labor and lives were fodder for their emergence not only suffer from their supposed inherent deficiencies but also from an apparent lack of gratitude for the privilege of having some part in this self-congratulatory portrait.

Tillotson points to the many contradictions and double standards of the neoconservative position, including its proponents' lack of memory of the role they played in creating the circumstances they criticize. The decimation of public institutions from the Reagan administration onward, for instance, created dysfunction on a scale that made it appear foolish to seek public solutions to problems of the common weal. At the same time, the bloated military budgets are premised upon the use of public funds for private interests. We could call this what it is: welfare for the rich. That African American interests tend to be linked to a viable public infrastructure made African Americans a marked enemy of privatization. In some instances, African Americans were collateral damage, but in most cases, we were in the direct line of fire.

The neoliberal position is not as overtly blatant as that of neoconservatives. While they share the neoconservative fetishizing of privatization, they are concerned with preserving some semblance of human rights and democracy in the process. Thus, they are compelled to offer an alternative to the neoconservative mantra of pathological blackness. Instead, they present a conception of democratic life premised upon individualism, which makes the collective needs of a disenfranchised African American population illegitimate. Privatization demands an engagement with African Americans as neoliberals continued the neoconservative attacks on public infrastructure. For neoliberals, African Americans were at first more collateral damage. As it became clear that African American interests rested upon a model of democracy premised upon group or collective rights, neoliberal critics waged a war on African Americans in the insidious language of being concerned about the ultimate interests of African American *individuals*. That assault, ironically, received its greatest support in what at first appears to be perhaps the most paradoxical effect of the civil rights struggle: the recent assertion of post-racialism as supposedly appealing to the content of character versus the color of skin.

From declarations of the end of racism to those blaming African Americans for the supposed continuing of racism through our continued appeal to the impact of race and racism in American society, post-racialism is a potent ideology of evasion and silence. In post-racialism, continued inequalities and, in some cases, their radicalization are ignored in the face of a symbolic moral victory. This is a not a new development of neoliberalism.

A recent instance is the insistence of post-racialism in post apartheid South Africa. Privatization and individualistic conceptions of rights dominated post apartheid South African politics in Black face, as the recent leadership attests. Aside from the emergence of a very small rich Black elite, the indigenous African masses of South Africa live the nightmare of an abandoned public infrastructure, catastrophic unemployment, and silencing of their protest under the aegis of the moral weight of the monumental transitions of the 1990s. The logic that is missed by postracialism is the understanding of how racism, as a social practice, functions.

All social practices offer a logic of exceptions. Thus, there have always been individuals who were treated as exceptions while the groups to which they belong suffered under a crushing weight of prejudice and violence. In simple language: It is possible to love individual politicians, entertainers, and sports stars of African descent and hate Black people at the same time. Similarly, it is possible for the Tea Party mobs voicing their hatred for the president of the United States to have, as they have shown, their black exceptions to their vitriol. Nearly all anti-Black racists know of either one Black individual whom they admire as "not being like the rest," or at least imagine what such an exception would look like. For them, that exception is really a white person with a dark or slightly dark complexion.

This logic is premised upon a form of narcissism in which the exception is a projection of how the dominant society sees itself. Since, as we have seen, that image is self-laudatory, it is as an ideal self, and as we know about narcissistic projections of ideal selves, the only recourse is, in a word, "love." Thus, whether it is an appeal to a small number of supposedly exceptional Black individuals among the neoconservatives or the post-racialists, the response of a nation whose shameful issue is such that it would prefer to cover it over or, in bad faith, simply believe pleasing falsehoods over displeasing truths, the result is of valorized African American individuals at the expense of brutalized African American masses.

Tillotson has taken on the task of exposing the contradictions of these assaults on the spirit through drawing upon resources from what he calls the African-centered perspective. The work is necessary, as many among us continue to suffer the heat in what, as those prophetic voices of the musical group Third World so poignantly reflected, is supposed to be the shade.

LEWIS R. GORDON is Director of the Institute for the Study of Race and Social Thought. He also is Director of the Center for Afro-Jewish Studies and a Laura H. Carnell Professor of Philosophy at Temple University and President of the Caribbean Philosophical Association. Professor Gordon has written many works in race theory, Africana philosophy, postcolonial phenomenology, philosophy of existence, social and political philosophy, film and literature, philosophy of education, philosophy of human sciences, and a variety of topics in the public interest.

Preface

Since I was a small boy, in an elementary way, I wondered how the idea of racial difference became part of the natural human order. I often marveled at how this particular form of racialized advantage had etched and set itself in place in most areas of human activity. As I grew into an adult and through years of quiet reflection and structured study, I began to understand that this type of favored position was not derived from the natural flow of the universe, but was artificially created by machinations from the minds of anti-egalitarian European men and their transplanted loyalists. Like many of you reading these words, I question their right to do so. This work seeks to illuminate how dominative privilege was developed and maintained in America from 1980 to 2007.

There have been significant scholars (Akbar, 1984; Ani, 1994; Asante, 2003b; Baldwin, J., 1993; DuBois, 1994; Dyson, 2003; Goldberg, 1993; Gordon, 1997; Kardiner & Ovesey, 1951; Marable, 1995; Mills, 1997; Omi & Winant, 1986; Reed, 2003; Sutherland, 1997; Welsing, 1991; West, 1993; Wilson, 2005; Woodson, 2000; Wright, 1984) who have examined racism and African Americans. Yet, despite these works, people of African descent remain at the bottom of every positive sociological indicator in American society (Powell, 2007; Winant, 2001). Many African Americans are now considered to be in a state of irretrievable nihilism and the argument is being made that some members of this population have become comfortable with this reality (West, 1992).

The spirit of resistance in African Americans appears to have been reduced in many cases to mere compliance and acceptance of the quality-of-life inequities in American society. Questions of collective agency and self-determination for African Americans have taken a backseat to notions of individualized success and materialistic advancement. What is problematic is that this state of affairs has led many to believe that this is a form of manifest destiny for people of African descent in the United States. This work investigates the possibility that the acceptance of dominative ideologies normalized this reality in the hearts and minds of American citizens but specifically African Americans.

Since the forced relocation of enslaved Africans to North America in 1619, most African people in America have been engaged in a constant quest for agency. Consequently, ideas connected to agency such as self-determination, sovereignty, autonomy, and collective advancement have been central to the African American experience in America. In my view the contemporary influence of ideological domination on the lives of African Americans and its continuing impact on this population's historical quest for agency must be investigated in its current forms. While racism, prejudice, bigotry, and discrimination have become familiar terms in the lexicon of America's social vocabulary, ideological domination remains in large measure misunderstood, particularly at the structural, institutional, and systemic level.

There are significant amounts of academic literature concerning European colonial systems and American racism but there exist few scholarly contributions that focus specifically on contemporary ideological domination and its influence on African Americans. This work seeks to fill that void. Clearly, what is warranted is a critical investigation by an African-centered theorist, which will illuminate how ideological domination remains a significant obstacle for most African Americans and how this population's collective spirit of resistance may be neutralized by an uncritical acceptance of the corpus of ideas located in the Post-Racial Project. How contemporary ideological domination continues to grant privilege to people of European descent and to those African Americans who acquiesce to its objectives is at the core of the racial problem in America. One of the questions this volume addresses is: How did the current African American disparate quality-of-life indicators become part of the natural human order in the United States?

This work will examine how the current quality-of-life disparities between many African Americans and most whites was ideologically determined. This work will also highlight how many African Americans have been conditioned to accept this de facto hegemonic state without 21st-century wide-scale collective resistance.

There have been few authoritative scholarly works in the discipline of African American studies that singularly explore ideological domination and its influence on African Americans. Alternately, conservative scholars aggressively offer their views concerning the "problems" of African Americans: (Carter, 1991; Connerly, 2000; Dershowitz, 1994; D'Souza, 1991; Elder, 2000; Hughes, 1993; Keyes, 1995; McWhorter, 2000; Sowell, 2005; Steele, 1990; Sykes, 1992; A. Williams, 1995; J. Williams, W.E. Williams, 1987; Wortham, 1981). However, there remains a dearth of information that illuminates the meanings of the ideological forces that work against the collective agency of African Americans, specifically, from 1980 to 2007.

In the post-"Contract with America" conservative social and political climate a growing body of ideas that this volume terms the *Post-Racial Project* has symbiotically emerged to influence how African Americans think about collective and communal resistance strategies against domination. The Post-Racial Project requires critical analysis so it can be dissected and exposed to determine if it has any political efficacy for African Americans; or if in fact it is anti-egalitarian. This is what I intend to do in this work.

By domination I mean the exercise of power that was gained by the wealth from the period of enslavement that is expressed through European cosmology/worldview by Europeans and their American descendants. This power is used to develop ideologies and maintain institutions that historically have prevented the full expression of African agency. Included in this analysis are ideological positions that maintain advantage for those who serve a system of inequality between whites and Blacks in the United

States. This is connected to the Post-Racial Project in that ideas in modern thought such as postmodernism, essentialism, so-called colorblindness, the social construction of race arguments, and the resulting corollary assumptions located in victim blame discourse all aid the dominative enterprise on various levels.

In order for a comprehensive investigation into the influences of domination to have a broad impact and meaning, specifically as it relates to contemporary realities of African people, would require all African people in America to see themselves as an African collective. This is not the current reality for many people of African descent in America. African worldview as the basis for African American reality is often challenged by African Americans who define themselves as solely American. Consequently, two declarations must be acknowledged in this work: (1) domination exists, which is demonstrated by the disparities in the major quality-of-life indicators between Blacks and whites in America, and (2) the collective sense of agency among African Americans has been and is being diminished by ideological domination.

Acknowledgements

No book is written by one set of hands and this text is no exception. I would like to thank Kassahun Checole and Africa World Press for its commitment to publish the work of African-centered thinkers. To my editor Angela Ajayi it was great working with you. Your attention to detail is without peer and I wish you well in your new endeavors. I am grateful to Dr. Marcia Sutherland who led me to the beauty of peace that can be attained by reading and quiet introspection. I will always be indebted to you for introducing me to the world of scholarly research and engagement that replaced my disappointment with the state of the world and its disposition towards people of African descent. I owe more than can be said here to Dr. Serie McDougal who has always inspired me to work hard and try to match his effort which is impossible to do, but nonetheless I try. I would not be here in this space if it were not for the kind benevolence of Dr. John Ryan whose unyielding faith and friendship has seen me through times that only his support could have changed and brought me forward in the light. This work is a product of the passion of Dr. Molefi Kete Asante who taught me the value of victorius consciousness and through his patient, and determined efforts at changing the world I bear witness to his courage as I set out to write for our people. I will always be appreciative of Ms. Mary Thorpe and Dr. Ralph Fitzpatrick of the Upward Bound Program for allowing me the privilege of working with the children. I know it was the children that pointed me straight in the moment and motivated me to think of their future. To the African World, those born and yet to be born I say thank you.

Introduction

This volume examines the relationship between ideological domination and its influence on the contemporary lives of African Americans. After a careful review of the literature, I have found few works that adequately addressed this issue specifically. However, there are a number of works that have dealt with racism, prejudice, bigotry, and discrimination as it affects the lives of African Americans.

Scholars (Asante, 2006; Baldwin, 1985; Kambon, 1998; Sutherland, 1997) maintain that African people are most healthy when they operate from within their indigenous cosmological and worldview paradigms. This idea will serve as the foundation for this work's investigation concerning the imposition of the European worldview construct and its influence on African Americans. Kambon (1998) is steadfast when he states, "... because if we are within our own "natural/indigenous" group culture and living only under our own cultural reality (and normally we are), then it is naturally our own group's (culture's) conception of reality that we are operating out of" (p. 119). Asante (2006) has addressed this reality as: "The Afrocentric Idea is essentially about location. Because Africans have been moved off of our own cultural and historical terms, decentered by the conditions of oppression, it is important that any assessment of the African condition or analysis of African phenomena be made Afrocentrically" (p. 152).

Sutherland (1997) speaks to the idea of African people being rooted in their own cultural realities in order to thrive and function. She asserts:

In the preceding chapters I discussed how people of African descent's dependency on alien Western cultural traditions such as selfish individualism, wanton acquisitiveness, and the repudiation of the sacredness of Black existence have contributed to the present cultural denouement and underdevelopment of the African world. (p. 125)

Psychologists White and Parham (1990) argue, "It is our belief that the personality, consciousness, and the core identity of Black people are African in nature. Whether conscious or unconscious, the personality manifests itself in the attitudes, feelings, behaviors, and spiritual essence of African-Americans" (p. 43).

J. A. Baldwin (1985) writes:

> This core component of the black personality represents the conscious level expression of the "oneness of being" communal phenomenology which characterizes the fundamental self-extension orientation of African people. While the African Self-Consciousness system is partly biogenetically determined, it is also subject to social-environmental influences as well. When this core system of the black personality is nurtured developmentally as well as situationally through indigenous personal and institutional support systems, it achieves vigorous and full expression in terms of a congruent pattern of basic traits (beliefs, attitudes and behaviors) which affirm African-American life in the authenticity of its African cultural heritage. (p. 62)

The idea of African displacement and its lingering effects on African Americans realities must be considered as historian John Henrik Clarke (1991) does when he wrote: "When you take people out of the cultural surroundings in which they originally developed you take away part of their humanity. African people living outside of Africa are so obsessed with surviving under conditions that they did not create that they often lack a universal view of their condition and how it started" (p. 406).

The idea of taking African Americans away from their innate rights to self- sovereignty and cosmological position is examined by Wacquant (2006):

> America's first three 'peculiar institutions', slavery, Jim Crow, and the Ghetto, have this in common; they were all instruments for the conjoint extraction of labour and social ostracization of an outcast group deemed unassimilable by virtue of the indelible threefold stigma it carries. African Americans arrived under bondage in the land of freedom. They were accordingly deprived of the right to vote in the self appointed cradle of Democracy (until 1965 for residents of the southern states). And, for lack of a recognizable national affiliation, they were shorn of ethnic honour, which implies that, rather than simply standing at the bottom of the rank ordering of group prestige in American society, they were barred from it *ab initio*. (p. 95)

The notion that African Americans have no cosmology or worldview of their own outside of the American context is demonstrated by Gunnar Myrdal (1944):

> Among the groups commonly considered unassimilable, the Negro people is by far the largest. The Negroes do not, like the Japanese and the Chinese have a politically organized nation and an accepted culture to fall back upon. Unlike the Oriental, there attaches to the Negro an historical memory of slavery and inferiority. It is more difficult for them to answer prejudice with prejudice and, as the Orientals may do, to consider them-selves and their history superior to the white Americans and their recent cultural achievements. The Negroes do not have these fortifications for self-respect. They are more helplessly imprisoned as a subordinate caste in America, a caste of people deemed to be lacking a cultural past and assumed to be incapable of a cultural future. (p. 54)

Myrdal's misunderstanding of the significance of African cultural history and its impact on Africans in America is a point of contention with profound implications. Myrdal does not emphasize the disruption of the enslavement period and its forced disconnection of African people in bondage from their cultural and historical roots. This reality has prevented many contemporary African Americans from having what Myrdal calls "fortifications for self-respect" (p. 54).

In the American context the ideas of Omi and Winant (1994) must be considered when examining the structural realities of African Americans and assimilation. They suggest that Myrdal believes that the only way for African Americans to make it in America is to completely accept a culture that is not their own. They argue that "Assimilation was viewed as the most logical, and "natural," response to the dilemma imposed by racism" (p. 17). This stance is against the idea that African Americans have an indigenous African culture that is worth keeping in America and the only way for them to be accepted is to completely adopt Euro-American ways of being. According to Omi and Winant (1994) "...Myrdal, drawing on the work of E. Franklin Frazier (as Daniel Patrick Moynihan was to do twenty years later) suggested that there was a "pathological" aspect to black culture which only assimilation could cure" (p. 17).

THE IDEA OF INTERNALIZED INFERIORITY

It is important in any study of domination to look at the idea of internalized inferiority that is displaced upon an assimilated group by institutional forces. R.C. Smith (1995) asserts, "An essential component of the ideology of white supremacy was the denigration of blackness" (p. 78). This is vital because it forces the African American into a position of having to choose value and currency in two places: (1) American culture or (2) African culture. Smith maintains, "...the black freedom struggle has always been twofold: to battle the structural conditions of material subordination and the psychological conditions of mental subordination" (p. 77). The notion of Black inferiority has long-standing and deeply rooted realities in America.

Introduction

In the United States the founders of the country and the framers of the documents that shaped the nation were not without their ideas concerning African people. Gould (1996) observes, "...we must first recognize the cultural milieu of a society whose leaders and intellectuals did not doubt the propriety of racial ranking---with Indians below whites, and blacks below everybody else" (p. 63). This type of reasoning is consistent with the history of racial prejudice in a nation that has demonstrated that conversion or even assimilation is not possible for people of African descent unless it serves the interests of the dominant class. The framers of the Constitution faced challenges when writing about African people. Thomas Jefferson once wrote: "I advance it therefore, as a suspicion only, that the blacks, whether originally a distinct race, or made distinct by time and circumstance, are inferior to the whites in the endowment of body and mind" (Gould, 1996, p. 64). This type of sentiment toward African humanity is shared by other thinkers of the time such as William Graham Sumner, a professor of political science at Yale University and one of the founders of American sociology. In the book *Race: The History of an Idea in America* Gossett (1963), is quoted as having once said, "...if you had asked Thomas Jefferson whether the statement "All men are created equal" was meant to include Negroes, Jefferson would have replied that "he was not talking about Negroes" (p. 154). Sumner (in Gossett) continues:

> If you should meet a man who would say...that all men ought to have an equal chance to do the best they can for themselves on earth, then you might ask him whether he thought the Bushmen, Hottentots, or Australians were equal to the best educated and most cultivated white men. He would have to admit that he was not thinking of them at all. (p. 154)

It is worthy of note to discuss the idea that according to psychiatrist Frantz Fanon, African people could only feel inferior in a place that was not their own. Fanon (1967) writes, "In practice, therefore, an inferiority complex connected with the colour [sic] of the skin is found only among those who form a minority within a group of another color" (p. 92). This statement speaks to the idea of enslavement as a displacing element in the lives of African people. Fanon's observation sheds light on the fact that Africans in America were forced into positions of self doubt brought on by the introduction to an alien culture and foreign worldview. In order to survive, the enslaved African had to adopt alien ways of being, which had to include a denunciation of even the basic elements of native Africa. The notion of American culture as not just foreign but "alien" is addressed in the work of Marimba Ani (1994). In the introduction to Ani's text *Yurugu*, historian John Henrik Clarke writes, "They have declared most things primitive that they could not understand. They have laughed at the gods of other people" (p. 1). This line of analysis was also followed by Ani who writes in her Glossary of Terms in *Yurugu*, the words, "Cultural Other" which she describes as "A conceptual/existential construct which allows Europeans to act out their extreme aggression and destructiveness, while simultaneously limiting their collective self destruction on a conscious level" (Glossary, p. 1). This operationalization is consistent with the documented history of colonization in Africa and African enslavement in America.

The mental dimension of domination must not be overlooked when examining the realities of Africans in America. Psychiatrist and researcher F.C. Welsing (1991) observes, "Inferiorization is essential to the process of oppression" (p. 243). She continues, "It ensures that the oppressors need not be troubled to hold the oppressed constantly under gun and key to keep them in the oppressed state; it keeps the oppressed from effectively challenging the oppressive process and system" (p. 243). According to Welsing inferiorization is

> The conscious, deliberate and systematic process utilized specifically by a racist (white supremacy) social system, as conducted through all of its major and or minor institutions (including the institution of the family), to mold specific peoples within that system (namely, all peoples classified by the racist system as non-white) into "functional inferiors", in spite of their true genetic potential for functioning. (p. 241)

Responsibility for Collective Ideas

The idea that African people must be responsible for their collective ideas will now be addressed. Asante (1999) maintains that many European and American scholars refuse to accept the idea that African people can produce scholarship that is relevant for African people. He examines the hegemonic framework that this form of domination exhibits. He believes that scholarship that speaks to any person's experience is best for that people and all of humanity. He emphasizes the notion that all people should have ownership of their own experiences and not be defined by individuals outside of the group. Asante's work is against any form of domination. Asante argues, "European control of space and time in publishing and the media has meant that legitimate intellectual and scholarly voices of African Americans are often not heard by whites who refuse to read African American scholarly journals" (p. 13). According to Asante, the writings and speeches of certain European and American scholars display an unwillingness to want to believe or accept the fact that Africans influenced Europe. Asante speaks to the critique of Mary Lefkowitz, a staunch critic of African agency, this way when he writes, "Lefkowitz has a curious use of language when it comes to the role Africans played in the lives of the ancient Greeks. She argues that there were "patterns of influence," but no real borrowing of Egyptian ideas" (p. 61). This passage makes the assertion that Africans have had no influence on world knowledge, especially as it pertains to Europe. One could reasonably conclude that this line of thought could lead to the suggestion that Africa has no worth, especially in the realm of intellectual production and thought.

L. J. Myers (1991) locates domination in the context of hegemony and oppression. She states, "The mentality that would be racist or sexist is seeing the world based upon a particular set of assumptions" (p. 16). This passage reveals a deeper reality for African people. It suggests a universality of assumptions that is imposed by Europeans on African people. Myers continues, "In a racist/sexist society, these assumptions or this less optimal conceptual system has become so hegemonous and pervasive that this lens used to view the world is often considered the only one valid or existent" (p. 16). Myers' analysis of domination speaks to the control of institutions that shape, form and frame the life chances and opportunities for African Americans in the United States. Myers' suggestion is that African Americans are forced into accepting and adhering to a set of cultural and cosmological assumptions that are outside of their native ways of being.

SELF-DEFINITIONS AND IDEOLOGICAL SHAPING

The relationship between Africa and African Americans' self-definitions and ideological shaping is not widely understood. W.W. Nobles (1991) speaks to this reality when he writes, "African Americans derive their fundamental self-definition from several cultural and philosophical premises which we share with most West African 'tribes'" (p. 47). This statement is consistent with the notion of Africa as the basis for African American self-understanding and knowledge of self. In the same article Nobles goes on to say:

> The notion of common experience or common ethos seems almost fictional if one accepts uncritically the research finding [sic] of many so-called Africanists who argue that the territory of the Western region of Africa held and still does hold within its boundaries many different "tribes," each having its own language, religion and customs. (p. 47)

Nobles' suggestion that Africa, while diverse, has common interests and customs is in concert with the thrust of the work at hand. African people while extremely diverse in Pre-Colonial Africa did have common cultural characteristics and ways of being that they lived by in large measure (Gyekye, 1987). If we accept the research of the major fields of science that have located early man as African, then it stands to reason that African people were the first to develop systems of organizing themselves in the universe. These organizing principles, in order to be effective and meaningful had to have some level of consistency across ethnic and so-called tribal differences in Africa so they could develop a cosmology and later on a worldview.

8

THE NATURE OF DOMINATION

The institutional nature of domination has been discussed by Asante (2005) when he addresses the role of the media. He maintains, "In Western heterogeneous industrial nations, the endemic nature of racism in the media is an inherent technological reality, as all technology assumes the motif dictated by its special mythological history" (p. 58). This passage explores the possibility that an institution (the media) has an agenda that is seen in how it organizes information, sends messages and gives value to certain myths. Asante continues, "An interacting racism networking the society leads a conspiracy of conscience against the best communication interests of all those who do not look like the corporate owners, producers, and directors" (p. 58). Asante is taking the position that the media have interests to serve and those interests at times do not in any great degree represent the well being of African people in America.

Asante (1998) addresses the machinations of domination and African people. He asserts, "In the spirit of pursuing the American quest, the Afrocentric idea is projected as a model for intercultural agency in which pluralism exists without hierarchy and respect for cultural origins, achievements, and prospects is freely granted" (p. xii). The Afrocentric idea speaks to the proposition that all humans should be able to own their historical and cultural experiences. This idea is not wedded to domination by positing all things African as the best for all people, but simply that it is best for African people because it speaks from and to their collective historical and cultural realities. Asante posits: "Thus, I offer Afrocentricity as a moral as well as intellectual location that posits Africans as subjects rather than as objects of human history and that establishes a perfectly valid and scientific basis for the explanation of African historical experiences" (p xii, xiii).

Afrocentricity is against all forms of domination and does not in its place locate Africa as superior to anything or anyone. Afrocentricity, is not the inverse of Eurocentricity which at its core is culturally chauvinistic, ethnocentric as well as xenophobic (Asante, 1999). Asante understands the centrality of having the African experience as the basis for African American reality. In response to those who believe that African Americans have lost their values (West, 1992), Asante (1998) writes:

> If we have lost anything, it is our cultural centered-
> ness; that is, we have been moved off our own plat-
> forms. This means that we cannot truly be ourselves
> or know our potential since we exist in a borrowed
> space. But all space is a matter of point of view or
> interpretation. Our existential relationship to the
> culture that we have borrowed defines what and who
> we are at any given moment. By regaining our own
> platforms, standing in our own cultural spaces, believ-
> ing that our way of viewing the universe is just as valid
> as any, we will achieve the kind of transformation
> that we need to participate fully in a multicultural
> society. However, without this kind of centeredness,
> we bring almost nothing to the multicultural table
> but a darker version of whiteness. (p. 8)

Asante is against any suggestion that African people are without values. He believes that if an African has no sense of urgency for agency then it must be because she is not living on her own cultural terms.

Particular Education

Most African Americans have been educated in the Western tradition in American schools and universities. The Afrocentrist is opposed to this idea because according to Afrocentricity this gives the voice of Europe all authority and power. Mazama (2003) illuminates this point about the nature of the Afrocentric idea as she maintains:

> The Afrocentric idea rests on the assertion of the
> primacy of the African experience for African people.
> Its aim is to give us our African, victorious conscious-
> ness back. In the process, it also means viewing the
> European voice as just one among many, and not nec-
> essarily the wisest one. (p. 5).

10

Mazama is asking African Americans to consider turning to Africa first for knowledge of themselves and then considering other viewpoints. Mazama's line of analysis is similar to another ancestral scholarly voice, Carter G. Woodson. Woodson made a similar plea to African people. Woodson (2000) believed that European education served the needs and interests only of the European:

> The Negro's mind has been brought under the control of his oppressor...When you control a man's thinking you do not have to worry about his actions. You do not have to tell him not to stand or go yonder. He will find his proper place and will stay in it. You do not need to send him to the back door, he will go without being told. In fact if there is no back door, he will cut one out for his special benefit. His education makes it necessary. (p. xix)

Woodson also argued that the African should be taught to see the world as it really is. He wrote, "What Negroes are now being taught does not bring their minds into harmony with life as they must face it" (p. 38). Woodson is speaking to the reality that because of domination, African Americans should be educated in a way that gives them some kind of understanding so they can best navigate and prosper within the anti-egalitarian structures as they existed at that time in world history and today. Woodson desired an African American educational curriculum that reflected the historical and cultural contributions of African people. He maintained with vigor that European/American educational systems were/are used to confuse and train African Americans to admire people and information that was completely outside of their own African existence. Woodson (1922) submits:

> Negro students are taught to admire the Hebrews, the Greeks, the Latins and the Teutons and to despise themselves and all other races which are now subject to exploitation. Whatever is is right. Nothing tending to question the present order of things is allowed to enter books adopted for classroom instruction, and teachers found discussing such matters are not tolerated. (p. 573)

Woodson addressed domination and made it quite clear with this statement: "The education of the Negro however has continued in the hands of the whites, the Negroes themselves being largely the objects of such efforts" (p. 573).

THE IMPACT OF DOMINATION ON THE PSYCHOLOGICAL OPERATIONS OF PEOPLE OF AFRICAN DESCENT

The psychological impact of domination on African people has been examined by several scholars (Akbar, 1984; Azibo, 2001; Harrell, 1999; Nobles, 1991; B.E. Wright, 1984). Their research suggests the possibility that domination has caused maladaptive responses in the behaviors of African people. Harrell (1999) states, "The healthy African self-conception is motion toward the collective" (p. vii). This observation dovetails with the research of Nobles, (1991) and Myers, (1991). They call for a sense of collective reality for African Americans based on the idea that African-centered traditions have the most value for African American people. The brain and its functional operations have received little attention by mainstream critical race theorists. The brain is the organ that controls behavior and so it is important to look at its importance in terms of how it uses and interprets information. Harrell (1999) posits:

> Tragically, the confines of racial oppression severely truncate the functioning of the brain. I have argued in earlier chapters that in service of the ends of white supremacy, images, ideologies, and events inundate the minds of the oppressed and cause them to belittle the African facets of their existence. (p. 166)

Harrell highlights the cognitive theories behind the "anti-African" sentiment that has been fostered in the minds of some African Americans by institutional domination. This capitulation forces some Africans to act outside of their native instincts and to see a disproportionate amount of value in other (European) worldviews that are reflected in their behaviors. The systematic exclusion of African contributions to the world stage and emphasis on European hegemony is not without consequence for African Americans.

Psychologist Bobby Wright, in response to this exclusion, operationalized a concept termed "Mentacide". Wright (1984) stated the following:

[Mentacide is]
> The silent rape of a people's collective mind by the penetration and perpetration of alien culture, values, beliefs systems, or ideas for the purpose of group destruction or political use of the victim group. Mentacide's method is to control; the behavior of the victim through mind control. Mentacide systematically utilizes the institutions which project images, values, beliefs and opinion's ...creating an illusion which the victim believes to be real until it's too late. (p. 12)

Wright maintains that as a result of the culture and institutions forced upon Blacks, a maladaptive psychological syndrome has developed in the minds of some African Americans. Wright examines the end results of the European hegemonic intellectual project and its possible results on African Americans psychology. Wright offers a line of analysis similar to Carter G. Woodson's. Wright's and Woodson's research suggests that through their control of the education process and its disproportionate emphasis on European contributions, individuals engaged in the process of domination have altered African American thinking about themselves and whites. Based on this research, the guided knowledge produced in the Eurocentric curriculum appears to have produced in some African Americans a certain type of negative psychological posture toward all things African (Asante, 1998; Hilliard, 1998). Based on this historical reality, one could argue that since the curriculum did not include the accomplishments, achievements, and contributions of African people that an imbalance or disconnect could occur in the minds of African Americans. Using Wright's analysis of "institutions" and their influence on the African mind it now becomes possible to understand the use of institutions as methods of domination.

Psychologist Daudi Azibo addresses the possibility that because of domination, many people of African descent have been psychologically destabilized and have developed behavioral patterns that reflect this. Azibo is concerned primarily with the psychological operations of people of African descent in America and their responses in an anti-African environment. Azibo (2001) writes,

> My interest in African personality stems from a longstanding personal observation that an individual African's consciousness of his or her Africanity and an African frame of reference (perceiving in an African manner) were pivotal correlates of effective negotiation of an anti-African environment. (p. ii).

He has developed a Nosology that explains the various states of disorder that may develop in the personalities of some African people. He asserts that these disorders are behavioral responses to white supremacy as manifested in domination. Azibo (2001) holds, "Psychological Misorientation is the most fundamental state of disorder in the African personality" (p. 84). Azibo's research reveals a reality that is often misunderstood. He continues, "I consider it to be the "basic Black personality disorder" in that it refers to operating without an African-centered belief system" (p. 84). Azibo's research is centered on the idea that the African personality is best served when it operates from within an African center. The centering concept is consistent with the writings of Asante, (1998) and Kambon, (1998).

The research of Kardnier and Ovesey (1951) seeks to explain the results of an oppressive environment and the black personality. Their project centers upon the idea that Black people in America have developed unhealthy personality responses because of the intense and unrelenting racist environment in which they are forced to operate within the United States. Speaking about the intent of their research Kardnier and Ovesey assert, "It is conceived and written on the premise that group characteristics are adaptive in nature and therefore not inborn, but acquired" (Advice to the reader, p. 1). This idea is maintained throughout the book.

The authors are convinced that most of the negative behavioral manifestations found in Black people can be traced back to the racist experiences and environments found in America. They go on to say, "Hence, the book does not describe Negro characteristics; it describes the personality he acquired while being obliged to adapt to extremely difficult social conditions" (Advice to the reader, p. 1). Kardnier and Ovesey (1951) contend:

> The psychosocial expressions of the personality that we have described are the integrated end products of the process of oppression. Can these be changed by education of the Negro? The answer is no they can never be eradicated without removing the forces that create and perpetuate them. Obviously, Negro self-esteem cannot be retrieved, nor Negro self hatred destroyed, as long as the status is status quo. What is needed by the Negro is not education, but re-integration. It is the white man who requires the education. There is only one way that the products of oppression can be dissolved, and that is to stop the oppression. (p. 387)

I disagree with the statement inside of this quote that states: "What is needed by the Negro is not education, but re-integration." I argue that what is needed for Blacks in America is a return to their indigenous African worldview, African cosmology, and African resistance theory with slight modifications to address current forms of domination.

A.N. Wilson (1999) addresses the notion of knowledge of self. He asserts that the healthy African mind has an understanding and appreciation of African value systems. Wilson speaks to the early Egyptian admonition of African people to "know thyself" (p. 48). He writes:

> We recognize today in Psychology that amnesia is a pathological state of mind; that a people who suffer from a lack of knowledge of themselves and of their history, a lack of knowledge of creation, are a people who suffer from a loss of identity. (p. 48)

Wilson's research and approach suggest an African frame of reference for the healthy psychological operations of people of African descent. The media and their influences play a role in the ideological domination of African Americans. Schiller (1973) examines the role of the media in American life. This research opens Schiller's lens and includes the media's specific influence on African American people. Schiller (1973) maintains, "The identification of personal choice with human freedom can be seen arising side-by-side with seventeenth-century individualism, both products of the emerging market economy" (pp. 8-9). Market economies and their power (non-conscious Rap music) on African Americans will be addressed later in this work. Schiller continues, "The view that freedom is a personal matter, and that the individuals rights supercede the group's and provide the basis for social organization, gained credibility with the rise of material rewards and leisure time" (p. 9). The notion of "individuality" is not reflected in African cosmology and is usually stated as against its basic tenets.

The role of print journalism cannot be overlooked when discussing the domination of African Americans. Allimadi (2002) examines this phenomenon. His research looks at what he considers the attempts by mainstream print organizations to use biased, racist, and oppressive images and stories to taint the image of Africans and Africa to the world. According to Allimadi his analysis is centered on how to "Fight the stereotypical racist representations of Black people and ignorance that still persists in contemporary media and the cover-ups that go with it" (p. 1). Allimadi contends his findings are part and parcel of a system of bias that is pervasive in America and distinctly connected to African American existence. He writes, "I have always been intrigued by the way the Western media have misrepresented Africans and people of African descent" (p. 3). Allimadi's analysis directs us to further critique. He states:

> There are powerful entities that benefit from the deep seated prejudices that have historically distorted Western media's representation of Africa. The racist characterizations justified and sanitized the crimes

committed against Africans, from slavery, through colonialism and through the new colonialism now maintained by the International Monetary Fund and World Bank. (p. 4)

POSTMODERNISM

Postmodern thought has emerged as one of the defining ideologies of the first decade of the 21st century and poses a threat to African Americans desire for collective resistance. Postmodernism is arguably a tool of contemporary ideological domination. Gordon (1997) asserts:

> I have always felt that if one were to scratch the surface of postmodernism, one would find conservatism under guises of bourgeois aestheticism and existential stoicism. Both turns pose no challenge to systemic orders of production by virtue of not engaging them in action or thought, the consequence of which is to leave the powers that be to their Machiavellian techniques of self-preservation. (p. 91)

The postmodern thrust is authenticated by the status quo ante to allow its values of European culture and dominance to continue unchallenged. Gordon maintains, "This concern about postmodernism isn't new. The ascription of neo-conservatism to postmodernism was a position Jean-Francois Lyotard attempted to refute in his famous postmodernist tract, *The Postmodern Condition: A Report on Knowledge*" (p. 91). Postmodernism is a threat to African American resistance because it demands fantasy. Callinicos (1990) makes the point:

> Foucault, more democratic, asks why "everyone's life couldn't become a work of art?" The answer, of course, is that most people's lives are still...shaped by their lack of access to resources and their consequent need to sell their labour-power in order to live. To invite a hospital porter in Birmingham, a car-worker in Sao Paulo, a social security clerk in Chicago, a street child in Bombay to make a work of art of their

lives would be an insult---unless linked to precisely
the kind of strategy for global social change which...
poststructuralism rejects. (pp. 90-91)

It is commonly understood, according to B.E. Wilson (2000),
that "Postmodernism opposes rigid class and essentialism to free
the self" (p. 68). The work at hand examines the possibility that
postmodernism is an ideological threat to the internal security
of African Americans. If absorbed wholesale by African Americans postmodernism is but another tool of domination because
if accepted uncritically it could reduce African Americans desire
for collective resistance. Wilson goes on to say,

> For one brought up to experience oppression, there
> must be an ego-loss; one must become an anti
> Oedipus. People of color everywhere have it within
> their means to throw off such an oedipal yoke. They
> have it within themselves to discover their conditions
> of possibilities so far denied by both the modernist
> and the postmodernist cultural forms. (p. 219)

DOMINATION IN THE 21ST CENTURY

In the first decade of the 21st century domination begins to
take a new direction. Haney-Lopez (2006) looks at this phenomenon. He asserts, "But to avoid breaking down, racial hierarchy
must also be newly produced and reproduced" (p. 144). This
assertion is important because it speaks to the new "morphing"
of domination in America. Haney-Lopez writes, "The greater
task, however, is ideational; new justifications must be elaborated
to explain the otherwise striking contrast between our public
commitments and our lived realities" (p. 144). The new ideas
and changing adjustments that are being made by those who
benefit from domination are in most cases hidden from common
people. These new realities are meaningful because they are the
new forms of domination that will continue to influence African
Americans. Haney-Lopez maintains:

> As a country, we enjoyed a very few years of civil rights reforms but continue to stagger under three decades and more of backlash aimed at preserving the basic parameters of a racial status quo itself built on the edifice of three centuries of White supremacy". (p. 149)

He takes his argument to the Supreme Court, the institution that Americans depend on for fair and balanced rulings:

> Colorblindness is frequently traced to the Supreme Court's decision in *Plessy v. Ferguson*, which upheld Jim Crow segregation in the South and prompted Justice John Marshall Harlan' famous dissent that "our constitution is colorblind, and neither knows nor tolerates classes among citizens." (p. 157)

He highlights the fact that "Harlan's dissent is today widely invoked for the proposition that the state should never take race into account..." (p. 157).

This work does not focus on domination at the level of personal racial prejudice alone. That type of singular analysis can be full of personal and isolated exceptions, which at times only serve to neutralize opposition to the status quo ante. A structural methodology is much more efficient and meaningful when examining domination. Goldberg (1993) asserts, "Structural methodology, by contrast, sees racism imbedded in, determined by, or emanating directly, even necessarily, from the prevailing constitution of social formation" (p. 92). The driving thrust of this work investigates domination in its ideological forms as they exist in American culture concerning African Americans. Goldberg maintains, "Racisms may simply serve ideologically to rationalize relations of domination, or they may serve practically to effect such domination by defining who are its objects and what they may be subjected to" (p. 95). Goldberg goes on to say, "Racisms may be taken most centrally and generally as the condition of this domination and subjection, the mode and fact of racialized oppression" (p. 95).

In the American context institutions have played a major role in the domination of African Americans. The highest court in the land, the Supreme Court, is not without its contributions. M. Abraham (2006) writes, "Countermajoritarianism refers to the ability of an institution to countermand or act against the predilections of a majority culture, particularly in an effort to protect minority interests" (p. 63). Abraham addresses the way institutions such as the Supreme Court actually serve the interests of a certain class of society, although this institution was designed to protect minority interests. The word "minority" speaks to the interests of the few and has no racial connotation here. Abraham contends, "On the other hand, the court has become utterly incapable of living up to its countermajoritarian mandate because of its structural dimensions, which will be examined in the course of this article" (p. 63).

The cultural structural dimension of domination is vitally important to its continuation. Cummings (2005) illuminates this idea:

> Conformist individualism works in a manner in which 'individuals' engage in aggressive competition with each other but to the extent that the system itself is threatened, instead any excessively aggressive tendencies are focused on the subjugation, consumption, and destruction of another culture/society/system. (p. 114)

This type of cultural system forces African Americans into another cultural identity that is alien to their indigenous African cultural systems. The idea of resistance has historically been a vital component of African American reality. Marable (1997) contends:

> "Blackness" or African-American identity, however, is much more than "race." It is also traditions, rituals, values, and belief systems of African-American people. It is our culture, history, music, art and literature. Blackness is our sense of ethnic consciousness and pride in our heritage of resistance against racism. (p. 195)

Marable is addressing a central component of African American life in America and that is the history of identity and resistance. An African person who is in an active state of resistance against domination is in a healthy state of mind. Marable (1997) continues, "This African American identity is not something that our oppressors forced upon us" (p. 195). Marable posits, "It is a cultural and ethnic awareness that we collectively have constructed for ourselves over hundreds of years. This identity is a cultural umbilical cord connecting us with Mother Africa" (p. 195). Marble highlights the connection of African American people and Africa.

A systematic examination of the influence of domination on African Americans must include a look at the beginning of the change from an "African" identity to an "African American" identity. The ideological conditioning process is historically known as "seasoning" and its aftermath is examined in this study. W.D. Wright (1998) argues:

> The British and white Americans were extreme in what they understood as their racial thinking with respect to blacks. They wanted the latter only to think of themselves through their color and race. They did not want their Black slaves, or even nonslave Blacks, to think that they had a beginning outside slavery or, as in the case of nonslave Blacks outside subordination. They did not want Blacks, slaves or nonslaves, to think they had come from some other part of the world, that they had had their own histories, their own cultures, prior to coming to North America. They wanted Black people, slaves and nonslaves, to think of themselves as being historyless, cultureless, and having only a color or racial identity. Another identity, a slave identity, was also emphasized, but the identity also had to carry the word *black* with it, and thus a dual identity of black and slave was created, but understood to be one single identity, with *black* and *slave* used interchangeably. (p. 30)

This form of identity formation /domination has contemporary applications and agendas. This understanding is critical if we are to understand the current behavioral manifestations present in many African Americans.

Many of the negative attitudes and behaviors of African Americans specifically young people in the current social climate can be traced to the influence of market driven non-conscious rap music. The various forms of nihilistic behaviors, anti-African self-presentations, value contortions, and negative identity formations in the Black community can be linked to the absorption of the European worldview in non-conscious rap music. West (1999) maintains, "Black rap music is the last form of transcendence available to young black ghetto dwellers, yet it, tellingly, is often employed to subvert, undermine and parody transcendence itself" (p. 483). West speaks to the grand narrative of music historically being a tool of deliverance for African people. He continues, "...black rap music is emblematically symptomatic of a shift in sensibilities and moods in Afro-America" (p. 482). West suggests a mood shift but, more important, a "value shift" that is predicated on the messages, motifs and artifacts expounded by non-conscious rap music. This specific art form is invested in and enveloped in the European worldview construct. The value shift and the resulting behaviors associated with them are the result of a profit before community psychological structure which is the result of an immersion in the European worldview construct by many African Americans.

African Americans engaging in this behavior are in violation of their ancestral responsibility bestowed upon them by virtue of the struggle waged by those Africans who came before them. Ancestral responsibility is the remembered sacrifice by modern-day African Americans to those African people whose blood, sweat, and tears made it possible for future generations of African Americans to move forward. This lack of ancestral responsibility is related to a value shift caused by the aggressive imposition of the European worldview construct found in the American cultural ethos.

Chapter 1

QUESTIONS OF EQUAL HUMANITY

Since the Ronald Reagan presidency of 1980 in the United States, there have been new challenges facing people of African descent, eclipsing the ideas of the Civil Rights Movement. Many Africans in America are now struggling to maintain the vestiges of what was left over from the mass movements of the 1960s; a collective struggle that was waged to insure equality for *all* of America's citizens. During the Reagan era a restructuring took place in human programs that included social, economic and political campaigns that were developed to reduce and in some cases eliminate equal access to resources and life opportunities so willfully granted to others.

The end result of these efforts was aimed toward a return to the American social order of the early 1950s and before. The Reagan administration planted the seeds and set the climate for what came to be called the Republican Revolution, which in 1994 would culminate with a document/manifesto titled *Contract with America*. Garrett (2005) argues, "The 104th Congress, of 1995-96, was the most important Congress of the twentieth century" (p. 11). While this statement is accurate for all Americans, it has particular impact for African Americans. The repercussions of this reality are discussed by Jansson and Smith (1996) as they assert:

> With a dramatic takeover of both houses of Congress accomplished in 1994, they focused on three strategies: (1) A seven year plan to balance the federal budget to force even greater cuts in domestic programs funded by general revenues; (2) "disentitling" of Food Stamps, Medicaid, and AFDC; and (3) large cuts in Medicare. (p. 445)

The 104th Congress set the stage for judicial changes that continue to reverberate in the lives of African Americans. These policies and practices are specifically profound in terms of the degree to which they influence the life chances and opportunities of African Americans, as will be explored in this chapter. Traditionally, the role of the U.S. Congress has been to respond to ideas introduced in congressional sessions and to make subsequent alterations of the ideas. The specific congressional changes are made to suit the tastes of individual members of Congress and their constituents (Garrett, 2005). The Republican-controlled Congress of 1995 represented the first time since 1954 that political conservatives would have control of the congressional branch of American government.

The radical conservative ideas of the Republican Party in the 1994 congressional elections were brought to bear in the Contract with America that was delivered to the American public on September 27, 1994, on the steps of the U. S. Capitol. The presentation of this document to the American people was not intended to be a one-day public relations event. It signified a distinct ideological directional shift for America. According to Gimple (1996, p. 17) the basic ideas of the conservative reforms located in the document were:

1. Individual Liberty
2. Economic Opportunity
3. Limited Government
4. Personal Responsibility
5. Security at Home and Abroad

These positions would alter the social, economic, and political landscape for African Americans in the last decade of the 20th century and in the coming millennium.

CONTEMPORARY CONSERVATIVE IDEOLOGY

According to Farmer (2006, pp. 40-48) traditional conservative thought is based on eleven basic tenets.

1) *Negative View of Human Nature*: Christian religious conservatives in the contemporary U.S. tie the negative view of human nature to the doctrine of original sin as based on the teachings of the Bible.

2) *Skepticism of Altruistic Efforts*: Traditional conservatives typically oppose liberal moral "do-gooders" and scoff at the efforts of those who attempt to improve the lives of the less fortunate.

3) *Emphasis on History and Existing Institutions*: Traditional conservatives argue that change, if it is merited, should take place gradually, come from experience, and occur within the bounds of existing customs and institutions.

4) *Society is in decay*: Traditional conservatives view the current society as in decay, depraved, and decadent.

5) *Demonization of Enemies*: Traditional conservatives also tend to demonize their enemies.

6) *Low Social Trust*: Policies for dealing with crime heavily emphasize retribution and punishment, with incarceration, corporal punishment, and capital punishment favored over rehabilitation programs.

7) *Return to A Better Vanished Time*: In order to return society to that better, vanished time, traditional conservatives believe that a good government resembling that of the past can be reconstructed as long as it is directed by good people with the correct set of values and the correct ideology.

8) *Government to Keep Order and Correct Human Weaknesses*: Traditional conservatives in the United States in

the last several decades pushed for laws to end abortions and favored laws against sodomy, pornography, prostitution, alcohol, and other "human weaknesses."

9) *Moral Absolutes*: To traditional conservatives, there most definitely *are* moral absolutes that can most definitely be known and practiced.

10) *Government to Support Societal Building Blocks*: In furtherance of their goal to create a good and moral society, traditional conservatives argue that government should reinforce the main societal building blocks of church and family.

11) *Opposition to Social Change*: In general, the adherence to moral absolutes tends to create a resistance to social change among traditional conservatives.

These ideas have served as the baseline definitions of contemporary conservative ideology and will be referred to throughout this work.

THE CONTEMPORARY CONSERVATIVE MOVEMENT

A casual perusal of the aims and objectives of the contemporary conservative platform makes it difficult to discern its dominative elements; but upon closer review it becomes clear what conservatives are trying to "conserve." The conservative ideology of today is keenly interested in returning America to the social order of post-World War II. American conservatism is deeply rooted in the conservative principles of Edmund Burke, an 18th century British conservative who was dissatisfied with the developments of the French Revolution and longed for the order of Anglo-Saxon traditions and institutions. Burke's English conservatism traveled to America in the minds of the emigrants of the New World (Micklethwait & Wooldridge, 2004, pp. 13-14).

One of the thrusts of contemporary conservatism is the belief in maintaining American institutions in their current operational status. To the radical conservative with their emphasis on history and existing institutions (Farmer, 2006) this connotes that Americans should accept the status quo which for African Americans means accepting white privilege as part of the "natural human order." Since American institutions were founded on principals set forth by landowning white males, this is consistent. America remains the only nation in the world that had at its disposal 246 years of unsalaried labor in the form of African human enslavement. The period of African enslavement in North America provided those involved in coercive labor the distinct advantage of benefiting from capital production without sweat equity investment. With the wealth gained from enslaving Africans, white males used the capital from unsalaried labor to industrialize America and design institutions to serve the needs of their interests.

The fortunes held from enslavement afforded the gentrified class of white males the capacity to build and construct not only institutional structures with brick and mortar; but equally important, it gave them the power to instill within these structures operational ethos. This institutional influence would later be reflected in their operational personalities. Having control of the social institutions would insure white privilege for generations to come. The Constitution was designed by the founders of America with provisions to make this possible. Beard (1986) argues, " The public good—the welfare of the nation—must be served, but it could be served best by recognizing that men are motivated mainly by desire for power and property and by founding institutions upon that recognition" (p. x).

Fundamental conservative thought and practice is deeply rooted in the Bible. Other schools of thought are directly challenged by the narrow constraints of conservative moral absolutist principles of God, country, and family. In the conservative arena ideas are a black and white equation with little tolerance for grey areas. Speaking to this reality Delgado and Gonzales, (2006) posit, "Neutrality is not an option...compromise is a sign of moral failing" (p. 120). The late 20th and 21st century contemporary conservative movement operates on political as well as racial principles that underwrite its policy and legislative agenda as Edsall and Edsall (1992) maintain:

Together, the twin issues of race and taxes have created a new, ideologically coherent coalition by pitting taxpayers against tax recipients, by pitting the advocates of meritocracy against proponents of special preference, by pitting the private sector against the public sector, by pitting those in the labor force against the jobless, and by pitting those who bear many of the costs of federal intervention against those who struggle for equality has been advanced by interventionist government policies. (p. 3)

These ideological wedges have been used to build alliances and to potentially separate poor African Americans from other segments of society in America. Ronald Reagan's 1980s supply-side economics had few positive outcomes for people of African descent in real terms. Supply-side economics is the conservative political theory which argues for, according to F. Thomas Juster (1982), "A reinvigorated economy with smaller but more effective public sector; and incentive structure designed to produce more effort, saving, and investment; a business climate more conducive to innovation and productivity growth; and a sharply lower rate of inflation" (p. 95). "Reaganomics" —the belief that supply-side economics and government deregulation of major industries would ignite growth, create employment, and "trickle down" to the middle class and maybe the black poor—turned out to be empty ideas that benefited only the wealthiest of Americans.

Reese (2005) contends, "Given the benefits they accrued from a strong military and tax cuts, corporations and wealthy families sought to balance the budget mainly through cutbacks on federal aid to the poor" (pp. 135-136). The conservative agenda called for a balanced budget and asked poor people to pay for it. Gonzales and Delgado (2006) maintain, "Today poverty haunts the ghettoes again ...the federal deficit has grown rapidly, while the economy as a whole has stagnated and jobs have dwindled or left for overseas" (p. 54). When examining the theoretical heart of conservative policies, ideological agendas become apparent that warrant investigation concerning the nature of their design. During his presidency, Ronald Reagan maintained that supply side-economics was best for America. The political nature of this economic position has been illuminated by Juster (1982):

> Seldom has an economic experiment been put in place with less conventional credentialing by professional economists. This is partly because supply side policies represent a political statement at least as much as an economic perspective, partly because aspects of the supply-side view of economic life are not testable by assessing their consistency with the facts of economic life; supply-siders argue that many such facts are irrelevant because they come from a world where important expectational forces were substantially influenced by demand-side considerations. (p. 95)

The lack of testability that economist Juster refers to is consistent with conservative ideas and their inherent inability to empirically argue their positions. This is true even when Juster promotes such ideas. To this point Juster goes on to say, "Entitlement programs have eroded work incentives; cutting back on those programs will restore incentives and reduce the tax burden on the working and investing population" (p. 95). The notion of "work incentive" is not measurable or testable, which makes it subjective even by Juster's own standards. Conservative economic analysis is at a loss to explain this issue; therefore conservative ideology relies on subjective value judgments because objective empirical information does not support this so-called work incentive position.

CONGRUENCY OF IDEAS

Both American political parties are articulating similar ideas but with different methods, as is illuminated by Bonilla-Silva (2001):

> Although the conservative camp believes that state policies cannot help minorities unless they are geared toward reforming their morals and culture and the liberal camp advocates for broad-class based social

policies that presumably will help everybody-but minorities in particular-both groups believe that (1) social policy cannot cure all social ills, (2) blacks deviant culture is a fundamental reason for their status in America, and (3) racism is not the central factor behind blacks contemporary status. (p. 8)

Bonilla-Silva goes on to say, "This convergence explains why under Clinton's 'liberal' administration conservatives and liberals agreed on all sorts of (universal) policy initiatives that have a disproportionate negative impact on blacks from so-called welfare reform to mending affirmative action" (p. 8). I am critically locating both, neoliberal and conservative racialized political/policy biases as contemporary ideological threats to the internal security of African Americans. I maintain that both of America's major political parties' initiatives as they stand in current policy platforms are anti-African American agency. Both parties serve to maintain the status quo ante, albeit with different approaches and designs. As Omi and Winant (1994) contend:

> This developing neoliberal project seeks to rearticulate the neoconservative and new right racial projects of the Reagan-Bush years in a centrist framework of moderate redistribution and cultural universalism. Neoliberals deliberately try to avoid racial themes, both because they fear the divisiveness and polarization which characterized the racial reaction, and because they mistrust "identity politics" whose origins lie in the 1960's. They want to close the Pandora's box of race. (p. 147)

What is unique about conservative ideology is its inherent belief that inequality is natural and has a right to exist among the human family. Farmer (2006) asserts, "Traditional conservatives view income inequalities as legitimate and natural therefore attempts at redistribution to the poor are a violation of natural order" (p. 41). The contemporary conservative agenda has shown little empathy for American society's imbalances—specifically, as they pertain to African Americans who are consistently located at the bottom of the major social indicators year after year (Winant, 2001). The conservative idea has historically resisted forms of government that were developed to balance society—from the New Deal of Franklin D. Roosevelt in post depression America to the Great Society programs of Lyndon B. Johnson of the 1960s. While Lyndon Johnson did not solve all of the challenges facing African Americans, he did offer historical truths concerning the past. In a 1965 commencement address at Howard University he said:

> But freedom is not enough. You do not take a person who, for years, has been hobbled by chains and liberate him, bring him to the starting line of a race and say, 'You are free to compete with all the others,' and still justly believe that you have been completely fair. This is the next and the more profound stage of the battle for civil rights.
>
> (Califano, J. A., Jr. 1999)

Johnson's ideas did not view inequality as the natural conscription of the human order. The naturalness of inequality that is ingrained and promoted in the conservative project can be traced back to the 19th century and English philosopher/sociologist Herbert Spencer. Spencer coined the phrase and developed the principle "survival of the fittest." The concept began as an alteration of Charles Darwin's theory of evolution, which Darwin developed to study nature's processes. Darwin's theory of natural selection was not developed or intended to study relationships between human beings, neither individual nor groups. Darwin's original work was centered on the study of animal and plant organisms. Spencer's reinterpretation of natural selection morphed into the theory of natural selection applied to social, political, and economic issues concerning human beings (Jackson & Weidman, 2004).

Herbert Spencer's view of the role of government was detailed in a pamphlet he wrote in 1842 titled *The Proper Sphere of Government*. Spencer viewed the role of government in two ways:

1. Government should be strictly limited to protecting property and person.
2. Government should not be responsible for education, building roads, or administering any form of charity (Jackson & Weidman, 2004, p. 76).

My contention is that these ideas are consistent with contemporary conservative ideology. The idea that social Darwinism is a stream of thought leading to and ingrained in the conservative project has been noted by others. Hofstadter (1955) maintains:

> In so far as it defended the status quo and gave strength to attacks on reformers and on almost all efforts at the conscious and directed change of society social Darwinism was certainly one of the leading strains in American conservative thought for more than a generation. (p. 7).

Social Darwinism is the foundational concept most present in contemporary conservative ideology, therefore I locate social Darwinism within the realm of domination ideologically.

WELFARE REFORM

During the Reagan era the racialization of welfare became a basic tenet of conservative political strategy. This administration ushered in the image of the "welfare queen," to describe Black women whom they alleged received a disproportionate amount of government-sponsored public assistance. Scholars have argued (Zizek 1997) that the iconography of the welfare queen in America situates the black woman as the "other" and bestows upon whites the ability to assume the position of virtue. This notion of public virtue actualizes itself in whites' desire to practice personal responsibility, which negates their need for any type of assistance from the federal government. Schram (2006) cites Zizek who contends:

> In the rejection of the social welfare system by the New Right in the US, for example, the universal

notion of the welfare system as inefficient is sustained by the pseudo-concrete representation of the notorious African American single mother, as if, in the last resort, social welfare is a programme for black single mothers-the particular case of the "single black mother" is silently conceived as "typical" of social welfare and what is wrong with it... (p. 210)

The racialization of welfare gave conservative ideology the self ascribed moral authority to challenge, reduce, and in some cases eliminate aid to Black women and children in need of temporary government assistance. Neubeck and Cazenave (2001) postulate:

The racilization of welfare did not happen overnight. For decades, well known U.S. Politicians like Barry Goldwater, George Wallace, David Duke, Robert Byrd, Richard Nixon, Ronald Reagan, Newt Gingrich, and Bill Clinton forged and exploited the link between "race" and "welfare" to such a degree that the two terms are now politically and culturally inextricable. Today, whenever politicians want to exploit white racist animus for political gain they need not say the words *Niggers* or *Nigras*, as did white southern segregationists. They now need only mention the word *welfare*. (p. 3)

Personal responsibility is one of the main tenets of the contemporary conservative agenda. This idea has special consequences for African Americans in both the private and public spheres. In 1996 President William Clinton's conservative ideological leanings urged him to sign into law the *Personal Responsibility and Work Opportunity Reconciliation Act* (PRWORA). PRWORA replaced the *Aid to Families with Dependent Children* (AFDC) program with the *Temporary Assistance for Needy Families* (TANF) program. The TANF program, put in place by PRWORA, yielded changes in the structure of welfare benefits, mandated time limits, strengthened mandatory participation in work-related activities, and altered many administrative approaches (Grogger, Karoly, and Klerman 2002, p. 3). In addition, the new federal guideline requires welfare recipients to perform waged work for a maximum of five years. This reform categorically ended AFDC. This bill replaced the federal statute that governed the AFDC program with a block grant that states can use to provide cash and services to low-income families with children, basically free of federal requirements on state program rules. This bill gives the states full authority to determine who receives aid without federal oversight. Without federal oversight, rogue states racial actors have the authority to arbitrarily choose who receives welfare benefits, which has led to disparities in levels of allocations between white and Black people.

In a study titled "Setting the Terms of Relief: Explaining State Policy Choices in the Devolution Revolution" by Soss, Schram, Vartanian, & O'Brien (2001), the researchers investigated the factors that led states to make restrictive policy choices after 1996. The research team used this analysis to evaluate general theories of welfare politics. Soss et al. contend, "The results of our ordered and binary logit models suggest that state policies have been shaped by a variety of social and political forces, but especially by the racial composition of families who rely on program benefits" (p.1). After media and political exposure to the negative images of Black women on welfare, many Americans internalized the idea that African Americans who received any form of government aid were indolent and without drive to better themselves and their dependents (Gilens, 1999). This reaction is not a new phenomenon and has a history in America. In 1960 in Louisiana, the American Civil Liberties Union (ACLU) argued that Louisiana welfare law was not conforming to the Social Security Act of 1935. According to Neubeck and Cazenave (2001):

> (A) statute, not discriminatory on its face, may be designed to deprive a single class of citizens of its rights to which they are otherwise entitled. Whether or not it is so designed, may be inferred from its impact. We believe the impact of the Louisiana statute can lead to the fair inference that it was designed to exclude a large number of Negro recipients of the benefits of ADC funds. (p. 76)

This bias is consistent with the findings of Lieberman (1998) in his work: *Shifting the Color Line: Race and the American Welfare State* he asserts, "Parochial institutions not only enabled but also invited local policymakers and administrators to create widely varying ADC programs that, in different ways, shaped the access of poor Black women and children to benefits" (p.118). By linking race and welfare, contemporary conservative ideological political discourse categorically defines African American welfare recipients as an aggregate population with inadequate core values and pathological cultural behaviors. Walters (2003) contends, "The true intent has not been to remove people from poverty–the real, but ignored issue in the welfare debate –but to end government assistance to them" (p.145). Walters' argument is consistent with the lived reality of African American life in inner cities and rural areas all across America. New rules on welfare reform have ordered African American women to leave their children and travel, usually on public transportation, to suburban jobs in order to retain the bare minimum in financial aid. This leads to in many cases, children being left in charge of their morning preparations for school as well as their evening arrangements for after school and bedtime.

The potential erosion of the African American family is not accounted for in the conservative programs aimed at welfare reform. President Clinton's signing of the *PRWORA* has profound implications for people of African descent in America. The ideological premises of conservative welfare reform are not consistent with the founding principles of America. Conservative welfare reforms are not prescriptive but punitive and serve to reduce the human agency of African American people disproportionately based on race and gender. Inscribed on the Statue of Liberty are these words by Emma Lazarus:

> Give me your tired, your poor,
> Your huddled masses, yearning to breathe free,
> The wretched refuse of your teeming shore
> Send these, the homeless, tempest tossed to me
> I lift my lamp beside the golden door!

Emma Lazarus' words are reflective of the American ideal. The conservative agenda is not consistent with the ideals of America because their versions of social policies contain anti-egalitarian racial caveats. These caveats, which will be examined in the next section, prevent conservative ideology from supporting programs and practices that extend a helping human hand to poor African Americans in legitimate need.

At the end of the 20th century and beginning of the 21st century conservative backlash has halted or stalled many of the ideas that freely assisted white European immigrants at the turn of the 20th century. Consequently, the contemporary conservative idea is contrary to the egalitarian principles of the American ideal that is written in the Declaration of Independence, which states: "We hold these truths to be self-evident, that all men are created equal, that they are endowed by their Creator with certain unalienable Rights, that among these are Life, Liberty and the pursuit of Happiness" (July 4, 1776). The conservative position that maintains skepticism to altruistic efforts in relation to humanity is noted previously in this work. The conservative notion of "skepticism to altruistic efforts" is not consistent with authentic American ideals of equality and justice for all citizens.

THE RACIALIZATION OF ANTI POVERTY PROGRAMS

The demonization of African American women who receive aid is symptomatic of a larger issue contained in contemporary conservative ideology, as Fording (2006) observes, "Although a number of alternative explanations have been offered, social scientists and commentators alike have increasingly cited the importance of racial stereotypes and the so-called racialization of poverty as at least partly responsible for the success of welfare reform" (p. 73). There are many streams of thought concerning the conservative positions on welfare reform but one hidden albeit intended outcome stands out, according to Barker, Jones, and Tate (1999):

> The conservative framers of the welfare bill argue
> that the five year limit was a necessary "tough love"

component that will ultimately benefit children. But lets expose this lie and be clear about who is actually going to benefit from the welfare reform act. Through its sizable reduction in the cost of the federal welfare program, and in passing off the future financial responsibility of the nation's welfare burden to the states, members of Congress and the President can pass the savings to the affluent in the form of tax cuts. And in 1997, they did just that. (p. 358)

The politics of antipoverty programs in the American context contain racial overtones that are lodged in conservative approaches to aid or aid reduction. The racial contextualization of aid in America is not a new phenomenon and this reality has not been lost on scholars as Newman (1999) posits:

In the intervening years, however, as many writers have noted, poverty has been racialized. Even though the majority of the poor are still white and working- as they were in the 1930's and thereafter-the public impression is quite clearly the reverse: poverty wears a black face and is presumed to follow from an unwillingness to enter the labor force. (p. 39)

A racialized conduit exists between conservative ideology and its formations of legislative public policy concerning the American welfare system and African Americans. Rooted in the American idea is the belief that all able-bodied people should work when possible and individuals are responsible for their own way in the world. In this regard Gilens (1999) comments, "For most Americans, then, interests and ideology point clearly in the same direction: welfare is a violation of America's cherished values and an unwelcome claim upon its economic resources" (p.1).

Conservative Americans are opposed to welfare because they believe it is disproportionately dispensed to the undeserving and able bodied. The question of "who" is undeserving is an area where conservative attitudes, prejudices, and politically inspired perceptions have taken root in contemporary conservative policy analysis. Watkins (1998) states, "Conservatives regenerated their cause and transformed American politics primarily by waging a deliberate campaign whose core themes often hinged on the strategic manipulation of cultural and racial symbols" (p.17). When dissecting welfare and its relationship to conservative ideology, conservative value judgments take precedence over sound empirical data when confronting this issue.

Historically, public attention to America's Black poor gained attention as an official result of President Lyndon Johnson's Great Society programs of the 1960s. These programs were developed primarily as social policy reforms with two of the larger areas being *elimination of poverty and racial injustice*. Public attention later grew into a critique of who deserved what in the eyes of the American public. Examining the welfare question in the 21st century leads to two focus directions:

1) Attitudes on public aid, and
2) Attitudes about the recipients of public aid.

According to Gilens (1999), attitudes are varied concerning public aid but generally Americans feel the recipients of aid are lazy and indifferent to work. Conservative attitudes also reflect a growing belief that African American welfare recipients have a natural propensity toward social pathologies that are unique to African Americans. Rector (2006) of the Heritage Foundations observes:

> Growing up without a father in the home has other harmful long-term effects on children. Children raised in single-parent homes are more likely to become involved in crime, have emotional and behavioral problems, fail in school, abuse drugs and end up on welfare as adults. (p. A17)

When looking back at the Great Society programs of the 1960s Gillespie and Schellhas (1994) wrote, "The Great Society has had the unintended consequence of snaring millions of Americans into the welfare trap. Government programs designed to give a helping hand to the neediest of Americans have instead bred illegitimacy, crime, illiteracy, and more poverty" (p. 65). Attention to the lack of conclusive data on this issue is brought forward by the Brookings Institution's Ron Haskins (2006) who maintains, "The evidence that welfare leads to more crime, more bad behavior, or more out-of-wedlock births is 'weak to nonexistent'. Nonetheless, the American public saw welfare as the root of many social ills and wanted change" (p. 17). Haskins' view is consistent with the findings of W.J. Wilson (1996) who asserts:

> The General Accounting Office (GAO), an investigative arm of congress, released a study in early 1987 reporting that there was no conclusive evidence to support the prevailing common beliefs that welfare discourages individuals from working, breaks up two-parent families, or affects the childbearing rates of unmarried women, even young unmarried women. (p.163)

Wilson (1987) goes on to argue, "Because all states have AFDC and food stamp programs, there can be no true test of the effects of welfare on family structure: there is no 'control' population that has not been exposed to these welfare programs" (pp. 77-78). The research findings of the Department of Health and Human Services, "Aid to Families with Dependent Children" (1998) (http://aspe.hhs.gov/hsp/afdc/afdcbase98exhib.htm.), demonstrates the broad diversity in the characteristics, race, and needs of Americas' poor; but this information is not reflected in conservative attitudes and language used to describe this population.

Based on the information produced by the government, contemporary conservative rhetoric does not match empirical reality (See Appendices A and B). To strengthen its policy platform on welfare reform, conservative ideology aggressively employed two types of social behavioral tactics: labeling effects and stereotypes. According to Jussim, Nelson, Manis, and Soffin (1995):

> Labeling effects refer to phenomena whereby perceivers' interpretations, evaluations, or judgments of different targets depends on the groups to which the individual targets belong (or seem to belong).

Applying a label to a target (e.g., homosexual, schizo-
phrenic, disadvantaged, etc.) often influences how
perceivers judge and evaluate that target. (p. 230)

In the early 1990s build up to the "Contract with America"
conservative ideology's target was African Americans and it relied
on racial fears to build its legislative constituency on welfare
reform. The process of labeling assured a two-tiered result for
conservatives concerning welfare reform. First it identified the
"other" and second it ascribed behavioral characteristics to the
target group. Black (1976) asserts, "One theory of deviant behavior holds that the labeling of a deviant as such makes him more
likely to deviate again" (p.117). This sentiment spread throughout the conservative movement and became a talking point for
conservative policy analysts highlighting the abuses of the aid
system. Stopping perceived welfare abuse was a common thread
in the conservative movement's call for welfare reforms. The
strategies employed by radical conservative ideology to achieve
its results are exposed in the work of Reese (2005) who contends,
"Meanwhile, Republicans gained popularity among traditional
whites—especially southern evangelical, male, and working class
whites—by constructing an emotionally powerful, racially coded
conservative discourse and championing policies that appealed
to nativism, racial resentment, and patriarchal "family values" (p.
133).

My contention is not that welfare is a natural good for African
Americans but it does point to the necessities, challenges, and
drawbacks of the system as W.D. Wright (1998) argues:

"Welfare" (or public assistance) is a primary means to
segregate and continue segregating Black people in
ghettoes in the United States. "Welfare" is a substitu-
tion for educating masses of Black people or training
them for skilled work or good jobs and also functions
simultaneously to keep masses of Black people out of
the job market as educated and /or as skilled labor
and instead holds them in place as a massive source
of cheap labor. Without the educational, financial, or

occupational means, masses of blacks have to stay put
in ghettoes. (p. 123)

However, in some cases as a special temporary intervention in
the lives of the poor, welfare can have life-saving value. Because
of the racialization of welfare by conservative ideology as well
as many so-called left-leaning progressives, African Americans
who utilized the aid system for short-term temporary assistance
as a response to unfortunate circumstances have been arbitrarily
criminalized as a group. This racialized criminalization is possible because race-related differences are not addressed concerning
welfare. Schram (2006) asserts:

> Such neglect is dangerous; it can ignore the systemic
> sources of poverty for low income families of color.
> Yet this failure is not just a conservative deficiency
> but part of a pattern of political inadequacy among
> liberals unwilling to discuss what they see as trou-
> bling facts about welfare recipients. (p. 208).

Welfare reforms under Contract with America and the
signing of (PRWORA) by President Clinton can be seen as a
reactionary racialized response to fears created by emotional
imagery based on artificially manufactured perceptions while
ignoring the empirical data pertaining to this issue. Attacking
welfare racially from the political position of high tax burdens
appealed to whites across social, economic, and political stratums.
This sentiment was particularly strong among working-class
whites in the southern states. Higher taxes and their purported
relationship to welfare resonated throughout white America and
fomented a widespread backlash against the welfare system. Poor
African Americans have been targeted by this doctrinaire position and held hostage by it in the public and political sphere.

This biased politically motivated reality finds its basis in a
flawed system. Lurie (2006) holds, "In fact, welfare policy is vir-
tually a case study of factors that contribute to implementation
failure: unclear and inconsistent objectives, intractable problems,
technical difficulties, inadequate resources, multiple implement-
ing institutions and constituencies, and the short time horizons

of responsible citizens" (p. 2). The ideas and understandings that many Americans developed concerning welfare were created with political intent. In her work, K. Sue Jewell (1993) explores cultural images and the shaping of social policy. She contends:

> The accepted cultural image of the typical welfare recipient is the African American mother and her charges. This negative and distorted conception is largely a function of assumptions that are made about the causes of poverty, namely the absence of a value orientation that includes the work ethic. This conception also includes racial stereotypes that characterize African Americans as individuals who devalue work and do not possess the intellectual faculties that are necessary to secure job skills, employment and the income to climb out of poverty. These images, definitions and labels attribute the depressed socio-economic status of African American women to the possession of innate qualities and the absence of a work ethic and other prescribed social conventions, such as a strong, viable family structure. (p. 21)

In this social and political climate, many white Americans accepted, uncritically, the politically inspired characterizations of African American welfare recipients. These publicly offered media-driven portrayals are not consistent with the empirical findings of the government document titled: "Aid to Dependent Families with Dependent Children the Baseline" (see Appendices A and B). Stereotyping of African American women and children receiving welfare became an accepted practice during the Reagan administration in order to insure reactionary voting for the conservative agenda, as Neubeck and Caznave (2001) observe, "...one way in which racial state actors and other European Americans have managed welfare policy discourse is through the use of controlling images that denigrate African American women, particularly their moral character and quality as mothers" (p. 32). The use of gendered stereotypes gave conservatives a distinct advantage over other political ideas because it set the climate by artificially creating an imaginary foe to rally against. Neubeck and Cazenave (2001) have examined this issue and they maintain:

> Politicians have blamed black mothers who must rely on welfare for nearly every social problem in the United States, including violent crime; the illegal drug epidemic; the decline of families, communities, and schools; the growth of rampant immorality; and even poverty itself. Black mothers receiving welfare have been cast not simply as prototype villains, but as a collective internal enemy that threatens the very foundation of U.S. society. They are portrayed as dishonest and irresponsible individuals who purchase bottles of vodka with food stamps intended to help feed their children, or immoral and promiscuous individuals who are said to rip off the welfare system for more benefits. (p. 3)

Conservative ideology consistently demonstrates empathy for white poverty which they maintain is usually caused by structural forces such as a recession or manufacturing slowdown beyond the poor whites' control, while expounding the idea that black poverty stems from a pathological aversion to work that is "culture" based. Freedman (2002) asserts, "Racial stereotyping and incorrect perceptions that families on the welfare rolls were overwhelmingly people of color were central in promoting public hostility to welfare programs over the ensuing decades" (p. 32).

THE RACE CARD

W.J. Wilson (1987) observes, "When figures on black crime, teenage pregnancy, female headed family, and welfare dependency are released to the public without sufficient explanation, racial stereotypes are reinforced" (p. 21). The stereotyping of black women by welfare reformers does not exist in a contained space. The description of black female welfare recipients as "breeders" by West Virginia Senator Robert Byrd in the 1960s laid the groundwork that set the climate for racial insensitivity that lingers and is inherent in conservative and neoliberal reforms (Neubeck and

Cazenave, 2001). The racialized images concerning welfare that are propagated by "reformers" are possible because of the history of the American enslavement period, when black women were forced to produce offspring for the plantation owner's labor demands. The "controlling images" that black feminist Patricia Hill Collins describes are useful when examining the conservative project because they are fixed in an African American historical context. Collins (1990) asserts, "If black slave women could be portrayed as having excessive sexual appetites, then increased fertility should be the expected outcome" (p. 77). Stereotyped imagery was employed in the public discourse surrounding welfare in the early 1960s and extend into the current discourse on this issue. W.D. Wright (1998) cites Jewell who maintains:

> The American public is regularly exposed to images of African American women as welfare recipients, procreating large numbers of children without the benefit of fathers who are willing and able to care for their offspring. Implicit in these messages is the message that through their welfare dependence, African American women are deriving benefits from tax dollars while others (white others) are being deprived of societal resources. (p. 124)

By locating gender and race in the same paradigm the conservative project often employs the racialized code term "welfare queen." This pejorative labeling locates Black female aid recipients as categorical abusers of the welfare system. This conservative linguistic coding system allows for public discourse to be racially charged without being overtly offensive on the surface. Ronald Reagan was not gender biased in his criticism of African American aid recipients. He was equally derisive of Black males in this regard. Derrick Z. Jackson of the Boston Globe reported that in 1976 while in Florida at a campaign stop, Reagan bemoaned "how hardworking people wait in line at grocery stores while a 'strapping black buck' purchased T-bone steaks with food stamps" (March 1, 2006, p. A.11 3rd edition). Reagan's spirit echoed prophetically for the conservative party. He energized the conservative electorate around this issue and galvanized support for welfare reform. During the Reagan presidency welfare reform became a major focus of the conservative project. African American welfare stereotypes rallied the conservative cause in the mid-1980s, re-gained steam in the 1990s and since has been used as a lure to attract southern white working-class voters who historically have been sympathetic to racially charged emotional ideas put forward in the segregationist political forces of the 1950s and 1960s.

The conservative movement's perceptions of poverty are manifested in their belief that they have no societal obligation to help the poor. This idea was articulated by William Graham Sumner in his seminal text, *What Social Classes Owe Each Other.* In 1925 Sumner wrote: "But we have inherited a vast number of social ills which never came from nature. They are the complicated products of all the tinkering, muddling, and blundering of social doctors in the past" (p. 118). He goes on to say "Society therefore does not need any care or supervision" (p. 119). Sumner was possessed of a long-term vision for American governmental policy. Contemporary conservative ideas on the role of American government and its citizens are consistent with the political vision of Sumner in 1925. Leaning on the racialized rhetorical tradition of staunch southern conservatives such as Governor George Wallace, of Alabama, Senator Strom Thurmond of South Carolina, and Senator Jesse Helms of North Carolina, contemporary conservative ideology criminally stigmatizes African Americans on welfare.

The conservative public discourse surrounding African Americans who receive aid does not match the empirically based research findings by the federal government. After examining the empirical government findings from 1983 to 1996 (see Appendices A and B) and analyzing the years 1993-1994, the data clearly demonstrate that contemporary conservative platforms concerning welfare and African Americans are a racially coded, divisive rhetoric that serves to ignite nativist fears in many white Americans. Conservative policies consistently ignore the objective statistical realities of welfare to galvanize the body politic for the advancement of their narrow political agenda.

WELFARE REFORM AND OUTCOMES FOR AFRICAN AMERICANS

The Rand Research Institute reports there is little information available concerning the effects of welfare reform on the use of other government programs (Grogger, Karoly, and Klerman, 2002, p. 13). Conversely, there is a growing body of literature that examines the positive outcomes of welfare reform (Bane and Ellwood, 1994; Haskins, 2006; Grogger, Karoly, and Klerman, 2002). However, the economic situation for most African Americans in the cities of America has worsened in the last generation. W.J. Wilson (1996) in his study of the contemporary urban poor maintains:

> In 1959, less than one third of the poverty population in the United States lived in metropolitan central cities. By 1991, the central cities included close to half of the nation's poor. Many of the most rapid increases in concentrated poverty have occurred in African-American neighborhoods. (p. 11)

Because of the impact of reductions in manufacturing and factory work, the United States has become a knowledge-based economy. This unavoidable reality must lead objective researchers to scrutinize and evaluate the role of education and its effects on the long-term quality-of-life outcomes of former aid recipients. Welfare reform does not address this issue adequately to date.

The literature suggests (Bane & Elwood, 1994; Haskins, 2006; Lurie, 2006) that conservative welfare reform has reduced the welfare caseloads in America. These observations lead to two fundamental questions that must be addressed when examining the aftermath of conservative reforms on the lives of poor African Americans:

1) Are former recipients earning enough to maintain self-sufficiency?

2) What is the impact of welfare reform on the ability of former welfare recipients capacity to pursue higher education?

According to the Governors Association 1998 summary of state tracking studies, between 50 and 60 percent of former welfare recipients found jobs that paid between $5.50 and $7.00 an hour (Lens, 2002). Lens reports, "Most recipients will remain below the poverty line even when working more than 30 hours a week" (pp. 279-290). New Jersey mirrors the common destiny of most former aid recipients. Two-thirds of former aid recipients remained in poverty after leaving aid rolls and one-third experienced severe hardship (Rangarajan and Wood 1999). According to Rangarajan and Wood, only one-third of former aid recipients had incomes above the poverty lines. These findings do not bode well for African Americans. In knowledge-based economies where knowledge and skills are crucial, poor people without access to education and training, specifically former African American welfare recipients, may remain minimum wage earners in various forms of menial occupations.

The minimum wage has not been raised since 1997, which places its real value currently at 1951 standards (Economist, 2006). Congressional bill H.R. 2, known as the Fair Minimum Wage Act 2007, sought to raise the minimum wage. The bill was strongly debated in Congress by both parties and eventually passed on January 10, 2007, by a vote of 315 to 116. The bill will increase the federal minimum wage by $2.10 an hour over 26 months, which represents the largest increase in the history of the minimum wage (Senate Republican Policy Committee, 2007). While neoliberal and conservative politicians consider this an improvement, the minimum wage will become the ceiling's end for many African Americans, because of the institutionally maintained restrictive covenants now entrenched in welfare reform concerning aid benefit payment for higher education.

In an article titled "Welfare-to-Work Proposal Would Limit Vocational Training," Dillonna C. Lewis, co-director of the Welfare Rights Initiative at Hunter College in New York, states, "HHS has narrowed the act and wiped out any possibility to use education as a way to qualify for work" (Chew, 2006). The proposed new rules would not allow welfare benefits to be used to pay for college. Elaine M. Ryan, deputy director of the American Human Services Association, states, "The narrower definitions of job training in the rules would reduce the ability of states to move welfare recipients into higher-education programs" (Fletcher, 2006). This idea, matched with the rising costs of a university education, will reduce the number of former welfare recipients attempting to enter college. This combination will lead to the 21st century reality of many African Americans being relegated to low-wage unskilled occupations.

The restrictions in welfare reform do not offer recipients aid in getting the education or training necessary to be competitive in a knowledge-based economy. Given the significance of education in knowledge-based economies like the United States it is doubtful that those without the training and skills needed to compete will be able to qualify for good-paying jobs. This reality is echoed in the work of D. Wilson (2007): "Employers want workers with literacy, numeracy, and information technology skills, to EPP, and Workfare jobs largely fail to provide these. Workers end up in dead-end, demeaning jobs that perpetuate poverty" (p. 44). This alarm was sounded earlier by Barker, Jones, and Tate (1999) who maintain:

> Many more single mothers on welfare lack the skills and education for jobs that pay a living wage, but the Act failed to provide adequate support for job training. Earning a high-school diploma or college degree under the new law will not exempt poor parents from the five year limit. (p. 356)

Opinions on welfare cut across political lines but lead to similar conclusions. In an article in the *New York Times* reported by Robert Pear and Erik Eckholm former President Clinton stated: "We took people who used to be the welfare poor, he said, "and now they are the working poor" (Pear and Eckholm, 2006). It has not been empirically demonstrated that a subjective so-called self-esteem boost can lead to an improvement in the quality-of-life for this population. In the same article Chevaughn L. Stephens of Seattle, Washington, a mother of three stated: "The emphasis on work first did not help me at all. It kept me back. It kept me from getting the education and skills that I needed" (Pear & Eckholm, 2006). The idea of putting people to work gets little resistance from Black Americans. It could also be generally agreed that working is an idea that few Americans would argue against but if it means creating a permanent Black underclass then this is completely un-American, or is it? Piven (2006) asserts, "...the Personal Responsibility and Work Opportunity Reconciliation Act of 1996 (PRWORA) has meant a restoration of the old regime in welfare and with it, the restoration of welfare racism" (p. 331).

For many poor African Americans, the reduction in quality-of-life outcomes that resulted from punitive welfare reforms are now a lived reality. This result was foreshadowed by Marian Wright Edelman in 1995 when she wrote:

> It is moral hypocrisy for our nation to slash income, health and nutrition assistance for poor children.... The Children's Defense Fund wants welfare reform. But we want fair reform that does not pick on and hurt children and that provides parents jobs and safe child care. We want reform that prepares our children for the new millennium -- not reform that pushes them back to past inequities within and among states. (1995, November, 3rd)

The current information suggests the possibility that the welfare to work reforms mandated by President Clinton with his signing of the 1996 *PRWORA* has helped to insure the beginning of a racialized caste labor system in America. This brand of ideology-driven social engineering will recycle poverty and possibly create a permanent African American underclass for generations to come.

The findings suggest that the racialized political rhetoric surrounding welfare expounded by the conservative project, and the policy reforms that followed, are anti-egalitarian in principle and in practice. The contemporary conservative project has attempted to categorically criminalize poverty for African Americans. The

1996 welfare reforms signed by President Clinton institution-alized a system of punitive measures that disproportionately affected poor African Americans. By reducing benefits for education and skill acquisition, current welfare reform guarantees that a new generation of low-wage Americans will be permanently fixed in low-tier employment occupations with little chance of attaining the so-called American dream. Consequently, the Republican-led rhetorical/political campaigns that led to the Contract with America were racially inspired and are not accurate reflections of reality based upon reviews of existing government data. D. Wilson (2007) sums up the Reagan era along with the current conservative policy initiatives this way when examining their impact on the conditions of poor African Americans: "Residents in these communities have been devastated by this. Growing numbers of desperately poor and dispirited people now struggle to make lives within new institutional and economic circumstances: trapping Workfare programs, low-wage dead-end jobs..." (p. 147).

The Reagan-era ideological platforms and their leftover policy manifestations reflected in current conservative American legislative initiatives have tainted the promise of human harmony in America. In the public and private sphere in America it is hard to avoid this reality. The Declaration of Independence's egalitarian spirit of concern for equality and equity for all of America's citizens will be historical footnotes thanks to radical contemporary conservative ideology. Radical contemporary conservative policy initiatives guarantee that the ideals of American democracy and full participation may never be fully realized for poor African Americans. For contemporary conservatives, egalitarian ideals remain an unpleasant human error lodged and locked in the 1960s. Because of its basic philosophical tenets, conservative ideology has destroyed to a large degree any efforts at an equal playing field for poverty stricken citizens of African ancestry in America.

I appreciate the position that many Americans believe in the idea of equal access to opportunity for all, but also grasp the policy-related restrictive spirit of current conservative reforms and their impact on African Americans. Present-day conservative policy platforms are anti-egalitarian and inconsistent with the ideals of America. The following are the major failings and inconsistencies of the contemporary conservative movement for African Americans.

FAILURES OF CONTEMPORARY CONSERVATIVE IDEOLOGY

- Does not take into account: The economic, social-political legacy of enslavement, Jim Crow, and legal segregation, which renders its analysis ahistorical.
- Does not take into account: The heritage of wealth developed from 246 years of unsalaried labor. This wealth forms the basis of the asymmetrical white/Black power dynamic in America today.
- Does not take into account: How wealth from the period of enslavement was used to develop institutions that served the sole interests of Europeans and their American descendants.
- Does not take into account: The reality that by having control of social institutions, individuals working in their own ideological interests are able to structurally entrench biased operational personalities in the functionary capacities of institutions and therefore are able to pre-determine the life chances and opportunities of chosen groups

The major criticism of contemporary conservative ideology in this work is directed toward its racialized theoretical imprecision. These subjective positions result in insufficient clarity regarding its key concepts, which are doctrinaire, race-laden propositions that serve only to stall human harmony in America. The contemporary conservative movement is anti-African American agency and as an ideology it poses a significant threat to the internal security of African Americans. The aforementioned components of the contemporary conservative operation through intended or unintended consequences reduce the agency of African Americans. The conservative movement is antithetical to the interests of Africans in America. Through its racially coded welfare reform and restrictive policy initiatives, which include vast reductions in educational assistance, the conservative project by virtue of its policy initiatives is creating a permanent underclass of African American citizens. Consequently, certain elements of the contemporary conservative idea punish poor African Americans for realities they could not create such as de-industrialization, global economic reconfigurations, and the current welfare system.

Chapter 2

THE NEOLIBERAL/ NEOCONSERVATIVE ALLIANCE

There exists a symbiotic relationship between neoliberal ideas, the conservative movement, and postmodernism. My contention is that the quid pro quo of conservatism and neoliberalism congeal and create spaces through postmodernism for each to operate independently but interdependently and this reality is not lost on operatives in both camps. Conservatives are ideologically opposed to postmodernism's basic tenets, (anti-foundational, fluidity etc.) while conversely it serves their political interests by demonizing so-called identity politics which could reduce collective resistance by African Americans. Because the neoliberal position on racism/inequality is slanted toward a socioeconomic critique of class and not race, it partners with the conservative stance that argues that degenerative Black culture and in their view, its inherent pathologies are the root cause of collective Black marginalization and not race. The neoliberal admiration for free market economies and its emphasis on "individualism" also makes it a convenient bedfellow for conservative principles. Neither position accepts the reality that a strident spirit of anti-egalitarianism and its concurrent operational components—most notably racism, prejudice, bigotry, and discrimination have any appreciable effect on Black reality in contemporary America. I have termed this symbiotic ideological relationship the "neoliberal conservative idea" or NLCI.

THE NEOLIBERAL CONSERVATIVE IDEA

Locating postmodernism as a partner of the NLCI is vital in order to understand its influence on African Americans. For the purposes of this work, postmodernism will be defined by the work of Terry Eagleton (1996):

> Postmodernity is a style of thought which is suspicious of classical notions of truth, reason, identity and objectivity, of the idea of universal progress or emancipation, of single frameworks, grand narratives of ultimate grounds of explanation. Against these Enlightenment norms, it sees the world as contingent, ungrounded, diverse, unstable, indeterminate, a set of dis-unified cultures or interpretations which breed a degree of skepticism about the objectivity of truth, history and norms. (p. vii)

Historically, conservatism has not seen the world or the human condition as fluidly as Eagleton describes. Choi (1997) observes, "In point of fact, conservative writers throughout American history have viewed minorities consistently as inferiors who must assimilate to succeed in the mainstream of society" (p. 115). He goes on to say:

> For example, starting with Edward Ross and Gunnar Myrdal in the early to mid-1900's and and moving to Milton Gordon and Arthur Jensen in the 1960's and 1970's to Charles Murray and Richard Herrnstein at present, race/ethnic relations in the United States have been regulated by a racist ontology that culminates in assimilation. (p. 115)

Moral absolutes guide the thinking of radical conservatives. The postmodern idea resists notions of categorical barriers in social reality. This aspect of postmodernism is useful for conservative policies that frame their focus on the premise of "we are all Americans." Whether intended or not, postmodernism gives the NLCI space to maneuver and argue its policy-related rhetorical formations concerning race-neutral legislation. Traditional conservatism is opposed to social change. This opposition lends itself to the conservative push toward the maintenance of American institutions in their current state; or when they deem it necessary to serve their ideological interests, an institutional policy restructuring may take place as was done to welfare.

The nature of the symbiotic relationship between postmodernism and conservatism is noted by Gordon (1997) who asserts:

> I have always felt that if one were to scratch the surface of postmodernism, one would find conservatism under guises of bourgeois aestheticism and existential stoicism. Both turns pose no challenge to systemic orders of production by virtue of not engaging them in action or thought, the consequence of which is to leave the powers that be to their Machiavellian techniques of self-preservation. (p. 91)

Gordon's observation concerning postmodernism's allowance of self-preservation and the maintenance of the status quo ante is consistent with NLCI's basic ideological thrusts. According to B.M. Wilson (2000), "Postmodernism opposes rigid class and racial essentialism to free the self" (p. 68). Postmodernism, if accepted uncritically by African Americans, can distort their history and stall their collective agency. L. Harris (1995) maintains:

> It has been argued that postmodern concepts of the subject delimit conceiving persons as agents of resistance because of the importance that postmodernists place on inherent differences (P. Smith 1988). If, as I argue, the postmodern concept of the subject lacks a viable sense of composite self-identity, not only is it difficult to see how persons enthralled in postmodern culture could be agents of resistance, but how could they have the attitudes associated with the desire to resist? How could they feel morally indignant about

personally felt infringements and wrongs, let alone social wrongs? (pp. 377-378)

My contention is that for African Americans to position the African self as nonessential is a pseudo-reality that reduces African Americans' desire for collective resistance, which alternatively maintains power for the status quo ante. Asante (2006) asserts, "All human beings create their contributions to the world on the basis of their cultural foundations" (p.147). For African Americans historically, identity has served to ignite their sense of political agency as Williams Crenshaw (1988) maintains:

> History has shown that the most valuable political asset of the Black community has been its ability to assert a collective identity and to name its collective political reality. Liberal reform discourse must not be allowed to undermine the Black collective identity. (p. 1336)

It is the reality of identity that has historically given African Americans the internal constitution to seek self-determination that allowed them to strive for agency. Asante (1998) maintains, "Blackness is more than a biological fact; indeed, it is more than color: it functions as a commitment to a historical project that places the African person back on center, and as such, it becomes an escape to sanity" (p. 137).

Agency and Identity

The twin ideas of identity and agency are inseparable for African Americans in their pursuit of equality in the American context as A.N. Wilson (1998) posits, "Collective identity, consciousness, intentionality and solidarity are the key determinants as to whether a group recognizes the resources it has in its possession and whether and how it will use those resources" (p. 39). The abandonment of the African-self is possible only if one were to undo the historical legacy of anti-egalitarian European American domination, inflicted upon African American people. African

Americans, like all humans, evolved from a past as Norris (1990) writes, "Men make their own history, but they do not make it as they please; they do not make it under circumstances directly encountered, given and transmitted from the past..." (p. 34).

The antiracial and cultural identity position that postmodernism demands means African Americans must pretend that their collective histories do not have an enduring legacy in today's America. As Jung Min Choi (1997) maintains,

> Minorities are expected to forget the past history of slavery, segregation, mental and physical abuse, and other suffering that they have endured in the name of assimilation. Past history is deemed almost irrelevant. Instead minorities must conform to the "common culture," so that they can function as a true American. (p. 117)

The notion of a "common culture" that Choi describes is part of the hegemonic thrust that is present in postmodernism. The late historian Arthur Schlesinger best represents this idea. Schlesinger (1992) contends, "If the republic now turns away from Washington's old goal of "one people," what is its future?-disintegration of the national community, apartheid, Balkanization, tribalization?" (p. 118). He puts forth an argument located in nativism, cultural chauvinism and aggressive assimilation. Choi (1997) defines this as "The Inferior Race Thesis." He writes, "According to Arthur Schlesinger, allowing differences to mix freely will culminate in the "disuniting of America" (p. 116).

The alternatives that Schlesinger warns against are the extreme result of a mind-set that does not allow identities that are not "American." The disuniting principle that Schlesinger is concerned with could also be the result of America's citizens of color growing dissatisfaction with being marginalized for desiring a cultural place to call home inside of America. Irish Americans as well as Jewish Americans have been given this dual cultural and social space through their public cultural festivals and observed holidays without complaint. Postmodernism and Schlesinger do not disparage these groups for maintaining these spaces. In his text, *The Disuniting of America*, Schlesinger (1992) singles out African Americans for causing disunity if they consciously seek connections with their African origins. He writes, "Surely there is something a little sad about all this..." (p. 86). Schlesinger has not publicly written or commented negatively on the Jewish community for its adherence to its cultural history and religious traditions. In *The Disuniting of America*, Schlesinger did not disparage white ethnics for the observance of their historical legacies. As point of fact he calls for a particular type of American vision as Asante (1999) maintains:

> Schlesinger sets forth a vision of America rooted in the past, where whites, actually Anglo-Saxon whites, defined the protocols of the American society and white culture itself represented the ideal to which others were expected to aspire. He loves this vision because it provides a psychological justification for the dominance of European culture in America over others. In his vision there is little history of enslavement, oppression, dispossession, racism, or exploitation. (p. 11)

While postmodernism and nativism are distinct in their philosophical stances, they are very similar in their outcomes for African Americans if adhered to uncritically. They both ask the African American to abandon his ancestral ties to African identity for different reasons. One of the intended or unintended consequences of the postmodern idea is the collapse of appreciation for African Americans to be able to celebrate their distinct cultural history and identity without being labeled essentialists. The postmodern argument is similar to nativism because they both advance the position that either you renounce your African identity, assimilate, or are deemed an essentialist. The goal of "one people" according to Schlesinger, requires that all ethnic groups (except white ethnics) must abandon their past to assimilate into America. There is an inherent danger in African Americans abandoning their essential selves. Choi (1997) highlights this position when he paraphrases John O'Neil. Choi writes "O'Neil argues that forgetting past history is a threat to an open society.

Ignoring history limits the very possibility of having a future that embodies alternate social orders" (p. 117). To abandon oneself from ones history requires the individual to dislodge from their identity, as Marable (1997) asserts:

> "Blackness" or African-American identity, however is much more than "race". It is also the traditions, rituals, values, and belief systems of African-American people. It is our culture, history, music, art, and literature. Blackness is our sense of ethnic consciousness and pride in our heritage of resistance against racism. This African-American identity is not something that our oppressors forced upon us. It is a cultural and ethnic awareness that we collectively have constructed for ourselves over hundreds of years. This identity is a cultural umbilical cord connecting us with Mother Africa. (p. 195)

As Terkel's (1992) interview with African American Lucy Jefferson illustrates, "When people understand who they are and understand their history, they have more respect for themselves" (p. 32). The postmodern notion of negating the essential self has been examined by other scholars Asante (1998) writes: "I have been criticized as an essentialist, a bad thing to be according to deconstructionists. They believe that when one argues for certain characteristics of culture that constitutes a given community, one is taking an essentialist position" (p. 13). The characteristics of culture that Asante refers to are what history bestows upon a people. The historical collective that human groups have developed are what make them unique in the world. Asante goes on to argue:

> It is unreasonable to expect African Americans to divest themselves of culture when such unilateral divestiture is neither required nor expected of other cultural groups. Imbedded in the suggestion is a notion of power and hierarchy according to which only communities considered of low status are required to abandon their essential characteristics,

while others seek to preserve their characteristics for generations yet unborn. (p. 13)

When one examines the social-cultural operations of people of Jewish descent in 21st-century America, nowhere does one find this group being encouraged to abandon its historical identity with any great influence. As a matter of course a large segment of this community fights to sustain its traditions by the establishment of Saturday Yeshiva schools to inculcate customs and ancestral responsibility in their youth. In addition, high schools in New York, such as The Marsha Stern Talmudical Academy, and many universities have some form of a Hillel Center for Jewish students to remain connected to their religious and cultural community when away from home. The Jewish mantra "Never Again" is made possible because of a determined effort by many members of this community to instill their essential culture, traditions, values, and customs into the socialization processes of their children. A.N. Wilson (1993) sees history as an important component for African American agency:

> History is what creates a shared identity in a people. It is based on that shared identity that they act collectively. To take away a people's history, to degrade their history is to degrade their sense of shared identity, is to remove the basis upon which they must behave collectively and reach their goals collectively. (p. 39).

THE AGENCY REDUCTION FORMATION

By locating group identity as a pejorative behavior postmodernism allows established Anglo-Saxon cultural structures and narratives to remain the universal standard by which all is judged. Therefore, I am advancing a conceptual counterargument here and locating postmodernism as an Agency Reduction Formation or (ARF). I am defining and operationalizing **Agency Reduction Formations** as: *Any system of thought that distracts, neutralizes, or reduces the need and desire for assertive collective agency by African Americans.*

Consequently, because the Black experience in America has been shaped by oppression, the fight against oppression is a key organizing principle of African Americans. Scholars such as (Appiah, 1992; Gilroy, 2000; Payne, 1998) have argued against cultural and historical identities, but conversely have made claims for human agency. These scholars appear to be confused about what identity has historically meant for African Americans. The forced migration of captive Africans to America was signaled by Africans being forced to abandon African identity and their traditions, values, customs, language, names, and even their idea of God. This process is being repeated many years later by postmodernists who are asking African Americans to distance themselves from their collective identity. There are curious similarities between the needs of the two epochs. Postmodernism as a social and political idea serves the interests of domination by virtue of its anti-foundational stance. Asante (2002) argues, "The problem here is just as the African has found identity after five hundred years of moving off centre, the West announces through post-modernists that there is no longer any warrant to discuss identity" (p. 110).

Clearly, the uncritical acceptance of postmodern anti-foundationalism by African Americans leads to a distorted sense of reality, which causes them to consider less assertive strategies for their liberation from the anti-egalitarian political practices that exist in contemporary America. Asante (2002) posits:

> The English is no more going to give up Englishness than the Tiger is giving up Tigerness. Suggesting the death of identity or the end of essentialism or the completion of the search for stability is nothing less than a betrayal of the oppressed. (p. 110)

The idea of eliminating racial and class boundaries as they relate to the betterment of the human family is useful. However, African Americans must employ a philosophical "skeptical realism" (Goldberg, 1993) toward the wholesale elimination of identity, because of the current unequal structural, systemic, and institutional practices in America, which render the postmodern concept in its current configurations unrealistic for African Americans to pursue. Goldberg speaks to the notion of skeptical realism when he states, "They are skeptical because experience has prompted a healthy disdain for extreme and untenable positions and for valorizing marginality without doing much about it" (p. 216).

I support Goldberg's position because it has yet to be seen or determined that postmodernisms basic tenets have made headway into the corridors of power in America, other than to suppress the potential agency constructs of African Americans. Asante's position on postmodernism is illuminating because he sees the postmodern project as an aid to the oppression of African people. Asante (2002) writes, "Afrocentricity rejects this as a false position, one that is intended to stunt the growth and development of African people while maintaining the dominance of Europeans as Europeans in a solid and stable place" (p. 110). Murphy and Choi (1997) employ Paul Gilroy (2000) to build on Asante's position. They contend, "Paul Gilroy aptly describes this situation by declaring that "European particularism [has been] dressed up as universal," thereby guaranteeing the success of a specific political and economic agenda" (p. 41). Postmodernism as a system of thought is incapable of placing African Americans in a position to advance their collective interests; therefore it appears to be an untenable social and philosophical position. Lucius Outlaw (1996) asserts, "Appeals to 'reason' have not been either an effective vaccine against the ravaging viruses of racism and invidious ethnocentrism or an antidote to the social ills they produce" (p. 12).

THE POSTMODERN CONDITION AND AFRICAN AMERICANS

Lyotard (1984) sees postmodernism as incredulity toward metanarratives (p. xxiv). According to Lyotard's view of postmodernism, the black experience in America is a metanarrative. This is a problematic concept for African Americans because the Black experience in America has been shaped by oppression. This is a reality for most African Americans at all levels of their lived experiences. The idea that the Black experience should be reduced to experiences that are not grounded in this group's identity is a problematic concept because postmodernism requires African Americans to abandon the collective truths that are inherent in their human histories that make them unique. This difference historically has been used to suppress the agency of Black people, but also has been used as a vehicle for group cohesion to deliver them from oppressive conditions such as the enslavement period, Jim Crow, and legal segregation.

The concerted focus on metanarratives such as racism/ inequality in the Black experience in America is what gave the civil rights period its energy and trajectory. In some respects, the postmodern call for suspicion of metanarratives has the potential to neutralize African Americans' desire for self-determining activities that will insure their full humanity in America and the larger world. Looking at the dangers of postmodernism, L. Harris (1995) argues, "The concept of postmodernism, I argue, is associated with such a vision—a vision which renders the immiserated irrelevant and Blacks, in particular, as ornaments without agencies or resistance" (p. 371).

The residual effects of the aforementioned ideas is an attempt to create a social and political climate where African Americans are being socialized and conditioned to accept aggressive forms of Agency Reduction Formations such as postmodernism, colorblind ideology, and the social construction of race argument. Clearly, if these sociopolitical constructs are accepted uncritically by African Americans, they will neutralize their resistance efforts against domination and maintain the inequities that continue to exist between Blacks and whites in America. A misunderstanding of these ideologies may result in further fissures and fractures in the African American community.

However, a critical understanding of these issues will help Blacks develop an informed perspective that will help them to make enlightened decisions on public policy, legislative outcomes, as well as the election of public officials in the service of their interests. A critical comprehension of the agendas inherent in these ideologies places the African world in a position to move toward a more community-focused realism, which places its concerns first, before those of the larger world. This is the goal of agency for any people.

Consequently, the uncritical acceptance of postmodernism in its current forms by African Americas, as located within America's cultural, social, and political projects, has the potential to lead to a collective political passivity of African Americans. Choi (1997) delivers a sound observation when he argues, "Indeed, the asymmetrical social relationships endured by minorities based on differences in biological, cultural, or genetic factors, which have contributed to elevating particular cultures over others, can no longer be justified" (p. 120). Choi's observations are on target in this instance, but the solution is not postmodernism in its current configuration. In order to change the existing structures that promote the asymmetrical relationships that Choi highlights would require a radical change in the American institutional social structure. Radical re-distributions in wealth, power, and structural arrangements must take place for the ideas located in postmodernism to have meaning for African Americans. Choi goes on to say, "Once the veil of objectivity is lifted from the assimilation perspective; there is nothing to justify other than a supremacist ideology" (p. 120). On this point Choi reflects reality.

Conversely, I contend that entrenched power does not see a need to justify its meaning. After examining contemporary conservative and neoliberal American politics, the strategy of those individuals in positions of entrenched power can be located in five steps:

1. Locate the appropriate vehicle(s) such as welfare, crime, education, tax burdens.
2. Abrogate the entrenched powers responsibility for producing the conditions that created the problems.
3. Identify the population or community that is deemed culpable.

4. Develop media campaigns to set the climate for punitive measures to be imbedded in policy decisions and legislation.

5. Create the structural and institutional reforms that serve these interests.

Because of the nature of current systemic, institutional, and structural arrangements in America, the "veil of objectivity" has not been lifted as reflected in the disparate quality-of-life outcomes that currently exist between Black and white people in America. Choi (1997) illuminates this reality: "Therefore, in order to garner healthy race relations, a complete rupture with the past is necessary" (p. 125).

The aforementioned realities position postmodernism as a philosophical and literary idea that has not proven to be an effective tool against structurally entrenched power. Postmodernism speaks to human possibility and optimism but remains frozen in social spaces and does not engage the policies or legislation affecting African Americans. Dissecting the goal of postmodernism, Lewis Gordon (1997) writes, "... the consequence of which is to leave the powers that be to their Machiavellian techniques of self-preservation" (p. 91). African Americans have little power in proportion to their population size at the federal policy levels, which makes it unwise for them to abandon their collective identity. It is in fact this identity that has served to galvanize their push for self–determination and agency. Harold R. Isaacs (1975) spoke to this issue by acknowledging the role of identity and psychology:

> I believe it is possible to say that in all cases the function of basic group identity has to do most crucially with two key ingredients in every individual's personality and life experiences: his sense of belongingness and the quality of his self-esteem. (p. 42)

In the last chapter of his text *The Racial Contract*, C.W. Mills (1997) speaks to the lack of realistic human utility of postmodernism:

> I am in some sympathy with postmodernism politically—the iconoclastic challenge to orthodox theory, the tipping over of the white marble busts in the museum of Great Western Thinkers—but ultimately, I see it as an epistemological and theoretical dead end, itself symptomatic rather than diagnostic of the problems of the globe as we enter a new millennium. (p. 129)

It is my contention that if African Americans uncritically accept postmodernism, their need for collective resistance as well as the struggle for human equality will be neutralized and the current asymmetrical Black/white structural relationships that exist in America will remain unchallenged and unchanged.

Chapter 3

INVISIBILITY AND OTHERNESS

Another stream of thought connected to the Post-Racial Project is the social construction of race argument. Developed as a dominative answer to the increasingly fading biological deterministic position, the social construction of race advocates argue that race as a category or classification is not real and is a hindrance to the dissolution of the race idea, which they posit is a problem for the human family. In this debate there are two views: the scientific viewpoint, which is based on biological research, and the philosophical perspective. The prevailing view today is that objective biological races don't exist (Andreasen, 2000). According to Andreasen "The history of the race debate can be summarized by considering the attitudes that theorists have taken towards three incompatible propositions" (p. 653). Andreasen goes on to list these propositions as: races are biologically real, races are social constructs, and biological realism and social constructivism are incompatible views about race (p. 653).

The first section of this chapter will explore the proposition that race is a social construct and investigate its relevance to African Americans' well-being and agency. This section does not seek to prove or disprove either theoretical position directly. However, I will explore the argument's efficacy for African Americans and argue that the social construction of race concept is a contemporary ideological threat to the internal security of African Americans.

The social construction of race position is against human biological distinctions, which links it closely to postmodernism and its anti-foundational theoretical approach. This is contrary to thinkers of the 19th century such as Robert Knox (1850), who once said "With me, race, or hereditary descent is everything; it stamps the man" (p. 6). This was the prevailing sentiment in American life for centuries. Race was the driving idea inherent in the period of enslavement, Jim Crow, and legal segregation in the United States and still embeds itself in most areas of human activity today. The social construction of race argument has emerged as a discourse among academics who seek to transcend race. Manning Marable (2000a) contends:

> Our ability to transcend racial chauvinism and inter-
> ethnic hatred and the old definitions of "race," to
> recognize the class commonalities and joint social
> justice interests of all groups in the restructuring of
> this nation's economy and social order, will be the key
> in the construction of a nonracist democracy, tran-
> scending ancient walls of white violence, corporate
> power and class privilege. By dismantling the narrow
> politics of racial identity and selective self-interest,
> by going beyond "Black" and "White," we may con-
> struct new values, new institutions, and new visions
> of an America beyond traditional racial categories
> and racial oppression. (p. 454)

Marable calls for a restructuring of America in order to have a "nonracist democracy," as have many before him. He is basically asking those in power to relinquish their privilege to strangers in the name of racial harmony. He wants ethnic groups to abandon their identities, dislodge from their "self-interests," and he admonishes them to consolidate their common class interests to pursue social justice. Is this a realistic agenda for African Americans who live in a nation that currently wrestles with its legacy of structural and institutional inequality? There is no consensus on this issue but many scholars do not agree with Marable's argument. Winant (1994) highlights the work of Etienne Balibar, whose neoracism concept examines the new type of racism that Balibar asserts is positioning itself as anti-racist. Winant (1994) writes of Balibar:

> First, he says, neoracism has effectively rid itself of any overt adherence to racial prejudice or advocacy of discrimination. Second, and by far more important, neoracism has moved beyond biologism to an understanding of race rooted in supposed racial differences, a position that permits a far more flexible range of racist political practices. (pp. 100-101)

I am extending Balibar's argument to include the social construction of race idea as racist antiracism. The race as a "social construct" community desires race to be a negligible feature of American life; but I ask, how this is possible in a society such as the United States, which continues to operate on racialized terms? Additionally one asks, is this position wise for African Americans who in most cases can be identified by their pigmentation? Philogene (1999) maintains:

> Underneath that surface, however, race remains a core determinant defining the American culture, and continues to be the obsession it has always been. Whites acknowledge that Blacks are American and that in American society all members are to be treated as equal. Yet at the same time they cannot wish away the long history of racism and segregation which created such deeply rooted images of black Americans. (p. 11)

The race as a social construct position exists in the same questionable reality with postmodernism by calling for African Americans to engage in abandonment strategies regarding their race. The race as social construct proponents are engaged in a new attempt at an old aggressive assimilation idea that was successfully advanced in the early part of the 20th century for European immigrants, but was never actualized by African Americans because of the refusal of many Americans to fully accept African Americans as equal citizens. While the Civil Rights Movement garnered legal protections and voting rights for African Americans, the resistance to them being accepted as equal partners in America has not abated to the point where African American humanity and equality are unquestionable, although the election of the 44th president of the United States makes this case symbolically at best.

The concept of race as a social construct has been explored in the affirmative by scholars of African descent (Appiah, 1992; Marable, 1995, 2000a;) while dissenting voices such as Lucius Outlaw (1996) maintain that race is real and considers it a constitutive aspect of human populations. The notion that race can be semantically reconfigured to render it invisible does not realistically reflect the state of race in America, as Outlaw contends:

> On the basis of a revised philosophical anthropology that draws on an enhanced social ontology mindful of social collectivities, then, perhaps those who philosophize would not mislead themselves in thinking that the elimination of antagonisms tied to invidious valorizations of raciality and ethnicity can be facilitated by "lexical surgery" that removes race from usage and replaces it, instead, with references to say, "communities of meaning" as offered by Kwame Anthony Appiah or, as he has proposed more recently to "ethnic identities," since he claims there is no such thing as race. It is as though "something awkward or troublesome can be got rid of by the mere process of calling it by another name." (p.11)

Outlaw's observations grant the discussion of race as a social construct grounding, coherence, and raw reality that is not evident in its supporters. The idea that a benevolent American institutional structure will eventually accept the social construction of race argument places African Americans in a precarious position, reminiscent of the mid-20th century. J. Owens Smith (1987) contends:

In short, the chief reason Blacks were unable to escape the slums, as did the European immigrants, has been the government has consistently refused to provide them with a system of protection that safeguarded their civil rights to enter into the mother lode of America's income redistribution systems. It has historically placed their civil rights to acquire property and to pursue employment and economic opportunities on the goodwill of their adversaries and competitors. These individuals have acted in the same manner in which Madison predicted in his federalist papers. They have oppressed the minorities. (p. 123)

Whether race exists as a biological or social construction, the consequences of it have material and political realities for African Americans. As Young and Braziel (2006) argue, "Race is more than merely fiction or scientific myth eradicable by the verbal fiat of a momentary academic disciplinary practice of a few theorists" (p. 7). Examining the material reality of this position, Lewis (2008) maintains:

W.E.B. Du Bois's famous pronouncement in the Souls of Black Folk, that the problem of the twentieth century was the problem of the color line, seems eerily appropriate, at least in this the first decade of the twenty-first century. Inasmuch as social science theorists would advance arguments that suggest we abandon the concept of race because of its imprecision or because it is ethically indefensible, the material effects of this phenomenon are as visible today in the United States as they were during slavery, Reconstruction, Jim Crow, and sadly, in much of the post-civil rights era. (p. 11)

Any form of Agency Reduction Formations place African Americans in the tenuous position of "minor/beggar." The position of minor/beggar is reductive because the agency of African Americans is stalemated while it waits for others to grant it permission to exist. Depending on the goodwill of "others" to advance African American interests historically has proven futile at best. I am not suggesting that interracial coalitions of the willing have not been successful in the past; however, in the current neoliberal conservative social, economic, and political climate that exists in America, it is not prudent for African Americans to depend on the sense of decency of others for their well-being. Orlando Patterson (1997) asks the question, "Why should the man who has enslaved and exploited you respond to your cry unless, far from being an immoral tyrant, he has more than a spark of magnanimity?" (p. 95).

The social construction of race argument begs the question, so what? So what if race is a social construct and not a biological phenomenon, how does this change the institutional, structural, systemic, and material realities for most African Americans? Rajshekar (1995) asserts, "On what level is a formerly despised minority likely to be accepted in such a society's ideological structures, which determinedly enforce hierarchy among its own members" (p. 9). The larger issue is if one were to accept the idea of race being a social construct then one must also acknowledge the consequences of this reality on the lives of African Americans. The race as a social construct argument makes the assumption that all Americans are capable of being moral persons. The static history of American race relations has not shown this propensity as Patterson (1997) asserts, "If people are not prepared to assume their own moral being, I am reckless to think for a moment that they will consider mine" (p. 110).

The current discourse on race from many black intellectuals is oftentimes argued without a full understanding of what it is that they are arguing for, other than the valid hope that someday race is not used as a barometer to gauge a person's humanity. In the text *Crisis of the Black Intellectual*, W.D. Wright (2007) illuminates this dilemma:

> Most Black intellectuals do not have a clear understanding of the phenomenon of "scientific racism" because they do not know clearly what racism is. Their thoughts, writings, and talk are overwhelmingly about race. But they also have their own bio-

logical determinism argument, one that is implied in their discussion of race and that they are not aware of, and one that they constantly employ. It is made every time they say that Black people have been oppressed and suppressed in America because of their race, or their color, and not because of white people acting as racists towards them. This argument makes the racial biology of Black people the causative factor, something that provokes white people to act in a peculiar, compulsive, and deterministic manner, and that causes them to abuse Black people. (p. 33)

The scholarly ruminations and pontifications of academics engaged in the race as a social construct debates' lack of conclusive empirical data, specifically as it pertains to everyday African Americans' advancement of agency, renders its positions less than useful in the real world of race and agency for African Americans. This argument lacks realistic applications for everyday African Americans because very few of the academics that debate this issue are inside of the institutions that possess the power to make the rhetoric a reality.

The dynamics of power are rarely discussed by the race as a social construct crowd and this is vital when looking at this issue. W.J. Wilson (1973) defines power this way: "Power ability-as the name implies-refers to the ability of group A to control or influence the behavior of Group B regardless of whether A has actually influenced B's behavior" (p. 15). Wilson's analysis of power is the central weakness found in the race as a social construct position. African Americans en masse do not have structural, institutional control or power to demand that others accept this argument. Specifically, African Americans as a collective community do not have at present the kind of influence on the policy apparatuses that could translate to meaningful change in the body politic and political economy of America. Wilson goes on to say: "In fact, the behavior of B can be affected by what it perceives to be A's power or power ability, and hence B is not likely to behave in a manner that will produce sanctions from A" (p. 15). In the American context, African Americans have historically and currently been situated in Group B, which would make it difficult to influence Group A (white people.)

The usefulness of race as it relates to power arrangements was illuminated by Ashley Montagu (1965): "It was and is a scheme of great utility, but it was and remains a highly formal system, an attempt to approximate as nearly as possible to the realities of things" (p. 83). It appears that this idea will remain lodged in academic discussions because it has not shown any significant degree of encroachment into the larger political world in a way that would benefit African Americans. Van Horne (1997) illuminates this point as he posits:

> Racial prejudice, racial hatred, and boorish racism persist in spite of scientific knowledge about the biology of race. They persist because of their social value and social utility. They persist because they are perceived to reinforce the safety, security and comfort of the familiar in the face of the anxiety, insecurity and discomfort of the unfamiliar. (p. 8)

This position is not a viable construct for African Americans because it relies on the benevolence and goodwill of individuals whose ideological tenets have historically resisted these types of humanistic approaches. I locate the social construction of race idea as an Agency Reduction Formation and maintain that it is a contemporary ideological threat to the internal security of African Americans.

THE COLOR-BLIND POSITION AND AFRICAN AMERICANS

One of the ideas that gained renewed momentum in public discourse in America in the last decade of the 20th century is the "color-blind" position. This idea is put forth by academics, politicians, policy analysts, pundits, and legal scholars who argue that America has no need for federally mandated protective measures for African Americas because America is now a color-blind society. Brown, Carnoy, Currie, Duster, Oppenheimer, Shultz

& Wellman (2003) assert, "Racial realists and conservatives think a color-blind Constitution means that public remedies to end social inequality between racial groups are illegitimate, the equivalent of "racial social engineering" (p. 32). The color-blind position also maintains that preference based on race is unconstitutional. The roots of the color-blind argument can be traced back to the legal argument for nondiscrimination and the idea of equality as related to American institutions and agencies of government (Kull, 1992).

The words "color-blind" were given life when associate Supreme Court Justice John Marshall Harlan uttered them in the 1896 legal case Plessy v. Ferguson. Harlan was the lone dissenter in this case; where the Supreme Court upheld the constitutionality of a Louisiana statute that demanded that passengers in railcars be separated by their race. This judicial decision led to the doctrine of "separate but equal "in America. Kull (1992) cites Justice Harlan:

> In respect of civil rights, common to all citizens, the Constitution of the United States does not, I think, permit any public authority to know the race of those entitled to be protected in the enjoyment of such rights. ...There is no caste here. Our Constitution is color-blind, and neither knows nor tolerates classes among citizens. (p. 1)

The color-blind idea is also represented in the Fourteenth Amendment, which centers on equal protection of the laws. According to Foner and Mahoney (1995), "The most important change in the Constitution since the adoption of the Bill of Rights, the Fourteenth Amendment established equality before the law as a fundamental right of American citizens" (p. 80).

The color-blind argument was the leading idea in the battle against racial segregation by proponents of civil rights from the late 19th century until the 1960s. The idea that agencies and institutions of American government should operate without regard to race is a noble one that America still struggles with, even with the passage of the Civil Rights Act of 1964, which outlawed segregation in American public spaces and major institutions. During America's Reconstruction Period (1865-1877) equality and equal treatment under the law were center stage in the political world for Black and white citizens. The history of legal racial segregation in America is underscored by decades of resistance from many European Americans who objected to the granting of this fundamental right to people of African ancestry in America. As Foner and Mahoney (1995) contend, "Few white southerners accepted the idea that African-Americans deserved the same political rights and economic opportunities as themselves, and some sought to reestablish a system of white supremacy as close to slavery as possible" (p. 11).

The resistance of white Americans to Black equality took many forms from civic violence to state-sanctioned mob rule as well as disenfranchisement. In the 1990s after the efforts of Herrnstein and Murray (1994) and their work in biologically determined, evolutionary racist ideology faded from respectable view, a new form of domination was re-energized albeit in a different form. So-called color-blindness has invaded contemporary areas of public policy such as voting districts, affirmative action, and school re-segregation as A.N. Wilson (1998) writes:

> The argument by conservatives on behalf of a new color-blind American society asserts that since the middle 1960's, we can talk only of an American racist past—legalized housing segregation, lynchings, segregated public and private schools—and no longer of an American racist legacy, in the form of persistent or vestigal attitudes, norms, and informal practices that prevail within a variety of institutions (economic, social, political) in our post-civil rights era. (p. 839)

Carr (1997) cites, Willhelm, who asserts:

> Throughout its history, White America adjusts its expressions of racism to accord with its economic imperatives and modifies its myths of racism to take into account the shifting economic circumstances... White America generates a new ideology to sanction

any fundamental alteration in race relations growing out of basic economic modifications. (p. 108)

Wilson and Willhelm's positions are illuminating because they demonstrate the malleability of ideological domination in contemporary America. Carr considers the color-blind position the "new ideology":

> The new ideology is "color blindness." Denying the existence of the African American is not new, as has been shown, it was made an integral part of the constitution by the founding fathers. What is new is that it became the dominant ideology when it replaced evolutionary racist ideology. As noted, it was started in the 1950's as a liberal ideology promoted by integrationist elites. Then in the 1970's, it was transformed into a conservative ideology using only part of Supreme Court Justice Harlan's 1896 argument for a color-blind constitution. This, in turn, became the legal rationale for reversing or undermining key liberal programs such as affirmative action, voting rights, and school integration. (p. 108)

The shape-shifting possibilities of the color-blind argument have profound utility for the maintenance of inequality as Brown et al. (2003) assert: "Color-blind ideology is no longer a weapon that challenges racial inequality. Instead it has become a powerful sword and a near-impenetrable shield, almost a civic religion, that actually promotes the unequal status quo" (p. 58). The term color-blind is powerful because it signifies an optimism that few would argue against but closer investigation uncovers a bias that is not in the best interests of African Americans as Winant (2001) argues:

> The successes of anti-racist and anti-colonial movements in recent decades are being transformed into new patterns of racial inequality and injustice. The "new world racial system," in sharp contrast to the old structure of explicit colonialism and state sponsored segregation, now presents itself as "beyond race,"

"color-blind," multicultural, and post racial. It seeks
to render racism invisible: it attempts to dismiss race
as a hold over from a benighted past, something now
well on the way to being transcended. It presents race
as a "problem" that is finally being "solved. (p. xiv)

Color-blind ideology requires a universal foundation to
be in place. Similar to postmodernism it asks marginalized
communities to relinquish their identity but it does not seek
to dismantle the universal that is European that is American
that is white. When looking at this as a set of metanarratives it
becomes clear what values are in the forefront, as Murphy and
Choi (1997) assert, "Because the metanarratives are assumed to
be universal, groups that most exemplify these ideals have had
enormous power. They have been able, in short, to demand the
subordination of those who are unfortunate enough to not have
these traits" (p. 2).

The call for essentialism comes from the color-blind proponents, specifically the American version, because they are
suggesting that the European American ideal is not particular
but universal. The universalism that they claim has a specific set
of values, traditions, mores, customs, and folkways that locate
color-blind ideology in its European American base. Thus,
color-blind ideology is color-blind, and appears to be blind to
people of color. This is the same universalism that was apparent
in the aggressive assimilation strategies of the early 20th century
and beyond. The term "melting pot" was appropriate because it
demanded that all non-Europeans in America melt or collapse
into the universal (American) way of life. American assimilation has always been an aggressive campaign to institutionalize
the European worldview into the psychological infrastructure
of African Americans. Assimilation demands that the person of
color make all the changes that bring them closer to the static
universal. As Murphy and Choi (1997) assert:

Finally, the tenets of assimilation are based on a
dualistic philosophy that is antagonistic to equality.
Clearly stated, assimilation reflects a racist ontology
where there are two separate ontological planes of

existence: white and others. Accordingly, the assimilation perspective is grounded on racist principles
where one group is automatically accorded high
status. (p. 45)

Two fundamental questions must be raised on the color-
blind position. Whose interests does the color-blind argument
serve? Is assimilation possible for everyone? Answers to these
questions are vital in order to understand the agenda of this ideology and its lack of utility for African Americans. Murphy and
Choi (1997) argue:

> The problem according to Herrnstein and Murray is
> that assimilation is not for everyone. Some groups
> are more assimilable than others. Depending on
> mental and physiological makeup assimilation rates
> vary. Even liberal theorists like Robert Park, have
> accepted the notion that blacks are hindered by their
> own physical or mental constitution. (p. 45)

The color-blind proponents make little mention of the "assimilation rates" that are possible for African Americans who have
outwardly recognizable physical differences in America. The
color-blind argument is an illusion that African Americans can
ill afford to accept. As Neville, Coleman, Falconer and Holmes
(2005) argue, "This response is an ideal to strive for if we, in fact,
lived in a society that was equal and just" (p. 29). I am locating
the color-blind argument as an Agency Reduction Formation
because it places African Americans in an untenable position of
agency surrender. Rajshekar (1995) contends:

> The net effect of these techniques has pointed
> towards a devaluation or disassembling of the com-
> munity structures of the African-American minor-
> ity, possibly leading toward their disappearance as
> a distinct collective or nationality, evidenced in the
> existence of thriving community structures and insti-
> tutions. (p. 8)

Color-blind ideology asks African Americans to depend on the benevolence and goodwill of white Americans, some of whom have historically been resistant to large-scale collective efforts toward African American agency. Carr (1997) makes the point:

> African Americans are not going to be dispersed among the White population. They are not an "ethnic group" that will be assimilated. They are not a "race" that can be made White by the pretense that people can be color-blind. They are an oppressed nation. (p. 141)

Color-blind ideology is detrimental to the well being of African Americans because it allows the current asymmetrical institutional relationships between Blacks and whites to continue. This idea was an effective legal instrument in the years of segregation, but in the current social political climate color-blind ideology is a weapon against people of color, as Brown et al. (2003) maintain:

> In rejecting race conscious classifications or remedies, the court adheres to a jurisprudence of color-blindness that made sense in the 1950's and 1960's when segregation was legal and was based on a rigid system of racial classification. Color-blindness undermined and transformed that system. But fifty years later when state-sanctioned racial segregation is illegal and people of color have still to achieve truly equal opportunity with white Americans, the color-blind ideal actually impedes efforts to eliminate racial inequality. (p. 58)

In its efforts to secure itself in the national body politic, color-blind ideology exposes its weaknesses and agenda as Loury (2002) maintains:

> Race-blindness, when interpreted so as to delegitimate actions needed to foster greater racial equality in contemporary American public life, is one expression of the liberal neutrality principle underlying the Anonymity Axiom. I will argue here that race-blind-

ness represents a superficial moral stance, given the historical situation, and that it should be rejected. (pp. 116-117)

The color-blind position has particular resonance in the Supreme Court. After the *Marbury v. Madison* case of 1803, the Supreme Court became the arbiter of the U.S. Constitution, the final authority on what the Constitution means. Supreme Court justices are in the unparalleled position of having lifetime appointments and salary protections, which grant them the opportunity to be objective in their decisions. The Supreme Court is also charged with the mission to declare acts of Congress unconstitutional if they exceed the powers granted by the Constitution. In state of fact, the Supreme Court should be the most color-blind institution in America because it relies on the Constitution to base its decisions. However, the Supreme Court is made up of men and women who have perspectives and worldviews that sometimes may affect their interpretations of the Constitution and reality. Supreme Court Justice Oliver Wendell Holmes (1991) once wrote:

> The felt necessities of the time, the prevalent moral and political theories, intuitions of public policy, avowed or unconscious, even the prejudices which judges share with their fellow man, have had a good deal more to do than the syllogism in determining the rules by which men should be governed. (p. 1)

Justice Holmes highlights the possibility that the decisions of the Court may not always be made by objective color-blind analysis. This should give African Americans pause for concern. The possible human subjectivity of the members of the Court and their rulings place African Americans at the mercy of its so-called constitutionally color-blind decisions. The Supreme Court is supposed to protect the rights of the "unheard and the unseen" (M. Abraham, 2006, p. 65).

The possible ideological subjectivity of the Supreme Court has not been overlooked by contemporary scholars. Abraham (2006) examines the Supreme Court and contends that it does

81

not always serve the interests of the minority as it was intended to do. He writes, "The U.S. Supreme Court, despite possessing the potential for exercising countermajoritarian discretion—in the protection of minority interests actually ensures the continual practice of what legal scholars call veiled majoritarianism" (p. 64). Veiled majoritarianism does not serve the interests of African Americans. Abraham continues:

> Veiled majoritarianism is a phrase that attempts to capture what legal scholars characterize as the promotion of majority interests through supposedly neutral legal principles that—while ostensibly promoting the goal of protecting vulnerable minorities against the "will of the majority" –give Supreme Court justices the discretion to inscribe their socialized belief systems into the law, all the while passing off such inscriptions as objective adjudication. (p. 64)

The neutral legal principles that Abraham refers to are being carried out by Supreme Court justices whose socialization and worldviews are supposed to be of no significance in performing their appointed duties. Centrist/liberal and conservative proponents of color-blind ideology may not be interested in egalitarian implementation of this position, but they are keenly interested in the appearance of color-blindness in the Supreme Court and other public institutions in America. The psychological and legal machinations that supposedly allow color-blind ideology any merit are the same realities that sustain power and privilege for non-African people. The notion of color-blindness is full of false optimism and empty hope but has no true bearing on bettering the lives of African Americans. This is the central assumption of this argument by both its Black and white proponents. In the current political climate the redress of racism is not met in most quarters with the same enthusiasm as the zealous push for the color-blind argument.

The color-blind advocates apparently see no correlation between the two. Proponents of the color-blind idea advance the notion that all of the questions surrounding race have been answered. Speaking to this issue, conservative pundit George Will

(2006) once remarked on, "the unbearable boredom occasioned by most of today's talk about race..." (p. 68). A second phase of "benign neglect" is surfacing because of the color-blind argument. Benign neglect was first seen in the policy prescriptions of Daniel Patrick Moynihan who was an advisor to the Nixon administration. Moynihan's suggestions led to a reduction in emphasis on welfare programs in the early 1970s (R.L. Williams, 1972). Moynihan (1970) stated, "The time may have come when the issue of race could benefit from a period of 'benign neglect.' The subject has been too much talked about" (p. 20). The argument that America is color-blind is empty unless it is structurally connected to the disparate material realities that exist between African Americans and others in America.

The color-blind position has not led to any visible changes in how society distributes goods or resources that benefit African Americans. These arguments are locked in the academic spaces of a few scholars who have attempted to carve out a special space for the presentation of their agendas. As Young and Braziel (2006) argue:

> It is a forced systemic adjustment of certain kinds of intellectual dissent, a shift toward epistemic closure, a locking out of the voice of the oppressed; but it does achieve for its elucidators a form of agency, a privileged space within the academy. (p. 10)

The failure of the color-blind argument lies in its inability to translate its meaning to the material world of African Americans. Marable (1995) illuminates this reality as he contends:

> But the question should be, how do we get there? How can we "deconstruct" race? We cannot get there by pretending that "race" and "color" no longer matter, that they have magically declined in significance since the 1960's. In a racist society, color symbolizes the inequality of power relations, the ownership of property and resources, between various groups and classes. (p. 125).

The color-blind argument perpetuates the imbalance of American society because it is being used politically to maintain the asymmetrical realities between Blacks and whites. Color-blind ideology has not shifted the balance of power in America, particularly who controls the political economy. I define political economy in terms of who controls the power to determine "who gets what, when, where, how, and why." L. Harris (1995) contends, "The possibility of African-American liberation from at least the ravages of racism depends, at least in part, on the acquisition of control over resources dictating material outcomes" (p. 376). An examination of the political economy is crucial when examining the reality of the impact of the color-blind position. Scholars such as: Appiah, (1992); Gates and West, (1996); Gilroy, (2000) argue in terms of desiring more harmonious human relationships and appear to articulate a self-emancipating tone, but these scholars rarely broach the subject of political economy or material reality. The role of economics must not be overlooked, as Asante (1998) asserts, "I must quickly add that the economic idea is, of course, a central creation of the interplay of cultural and environmental factors, and therefore contributes also to our way of viewing reality" (p. 136).

I support the argument by Young (2006) in an article titled: "Putting Materialism Back into Race Theory: Toward a Transformative Theory of Race." He writes, "By freedom, I do not simply mean a legal or cultural articulation of individual rights, as proposed by bourgeois race theorists. Instead, I theorize freedom as a material effect of emancipated economic forms" (p. 32). Young articulates a reality that many color-blind proponents do not. He calls for economic emancipation, not just an individual cultural tolerance, which locates his argument as a challenge to the current state of the political economy. Young brings the color-blind issue back onto firm ground as he argues for a material component to be part of the discourse. The lack of critique of the disparities that exist in terms of material realities between Blacks and whites by color-blind proponents is telling. They refuse to draw a direct relationship between race, racism and the political-economic structures that are driven by racialized ideological forces that affect the material life chances and opportunities for African Americans, as Isaacs (2007), observes:

> Economist Tom Hertz (2005, 2006) finds similar relative mobility patterns to those displayed in Figure 6. In fact, his analyses, which include all individuals in the PSID [Panel Study of Income Dynamics] who were born between 1942 and 1972, show even larger racial disparities, particularly with regard to black children being trapped in the bottom of the income distribution. From this pattern, he concludes that much of the overall intergenerational persistence of poverty in America is driven by the experience of black children. More generally, he argues that a key channel for the overall transmission of economic status from parents to children in the United States is the passing down of skin color and other characteristics that are correlated with race and that have social and economic consequences for their children. (p. 11)

Asante (2006) brings a tight focus to the color-blind position taken by scholars of African descent. Asante contends that Black scholars who argue most stridently for the color-blind position may have the desire to abandon their past. He says, "Only those who have a need to escape from their own histories have a need for such a raceless future" (p. 153). He goes on to illuminate a plan of action that would be more realistic and meaningful for the color-blind proponents: "On the contrary, it is much more helpful that we defeat the notion of racial inferiority and establish a broad new moral vision based on mutual respect for all human beings" (p. 153). The color-blind argument calls for an end to collective identities but appears to be selective in which groups identities must be abandoned. Asante asserts:

> There is no assault on Jewish identity, as a religious or cultural identity, nor is there an attack on French identity or Chinese identity as collective historical realities. There is no assault on the historically

constructed identity of the Hindu Indian, or on the
white British. (p. 150)

The notion that African Americans as a group should be
singled out to abandon their collective history by color-blind ideology is reflective of the double standards and bad faith ingrained
in the arguments central tenets. The color-blind position situates
African Americans in the minor/beggar position once again.
This is where color-blind ideology distinctly exposes itself as
an Agency Reduction Formation. The suggestion that African
Americans should relinquish the concept of race is antithetical
to their interests because African Americans had nothing to do
with its development or its usage against them. Asante (2006)
critiques Gilroy (2000) on this point specifically:

> I do not know how Gilroy can move from this posi-
> tion to indict the African people as the carriers of
> this anxiety about "race," clearly a concept that was
> never promoted by African people in this country or
> on the continent. (p. 151)

When speaking to the idea of which group holds onto the concept
of race Asante contends, "It is essentially an Anglo-Germanic
notion, manufactured and disseminated to promote the distinctions between peoples and to establish a European hierarchy
over Africans and Asians as well as to define a hierarchy among
themselves" (p. 151). The notion that the concept of race is being
held onto exclusively by African Americans denies the historical context in which African Americans have fought against its
use. Replete in the historical record are numerous examples of
African Americans calling for the end of race being used as an
instrument of dehumanization against people of color. The anti-
lynching campaigns of the late 19th century and the protracted
struggle over separate but equal public facilities all demonstrate
that African Americans possessed the desire to remind America
that collectively they did not want race to be the sole barometer
of their personhood.

Color-blind positions like the ones taken in Gilroy's text
Against Race (2000) are hopeful but ahistorical. Gilroy writes,

"The pursuit of liberation from "race" is an especially urgent matter for those people who, like modern Blacks in the period after transatlantic slavery, were assigned an inferior position in the enduring hierarchies that racilogy creates" (p. 15). The singling out of Black people for this project by Gilroy may be indicative of an internal need for race abandonment (Asante, 2006). The call should be made to the individuals who created the idea of race, not African Americans who have been marginalized by its abuses. This line of reasoning displaces blame onto those who are considered safe to attack. This is a retreat position that asks the innocent to stop committing the crime. The objective historical record does not document the idea that African Americans have used their "Blackness" to dominate anyone. African Americans as a group have never had control of the social, political, or economic institutions in America that would allow them to enforce their Blackness on other groups. The notion that they should "let go" of their ethnicity is evidence of a deeper psychological need for one to gain acceptance by others.

Being Black and identifying oneself as such is not the problem. The responses to blackness from others is where the pathology lives, but color-blind ideology does not seek to address this phenomenon, it simply wants to get rid of race. To get rid of race would require a non-recognition of immutable human characteristics. Gotanda (1991) refers to this as dialectical logic:

> The inherent self-contradictions of nonrecognition can be summarized in terms of dialectical logic. A subject is defined by its negation hence, an assertion of nonconsideration necessarily implies consideration. The stronger and more defined the character of racial recognition, the clearer and more sharply drawn its dialectical opposite, racial nonrecognition. The assertion "I noticed but did not consider race" divides the dialectic into its two components, consideration and nonconsideration. It then focuses exclusively on the nonconsideration by denying the existence of the consideration component. While this is a complex maneuver surrounded by assertions of moral superiority, the attempt to deny racial

> consideration is at its root, an attempt to hide the
> underlying racial oppression, a realty no amount of
> wand-waving and obfuscation can eliminate. (p. 23)

Gotanda illuminates one of the central drawbacks of the color-
blind position for African Americans. There are two brands of
color-blind ideology in America. The first brand lives in so-called
enlightened academic spaces and insulated social arrangements
that are ordained by the participants themselves without external
structural influences when possible. The second brand inhabits
the neo-liberal and conservative political structures of America
that argue that America is color-blind according to the Constitution. Both brands maintain and uphold existing social conditions
as well as perpetuate asymmetrical institutional relationships
between whites and African Americans under the guise of race
neutrality.

This neutrality is doubtful because as Williams Crenshaw
(1988) argues, "First, racism is a central ideological underpin-
ning of American society" (p. 1336). The "wand-waving" that
Gotanda (1991) speaks of would have to be sanctioned by the
Supreme Court, advanced by federal mandates, and transferred
to state and local governments. These ideas would also have to be
lodged in day-to-day operations of America's major institutions,
which is no guarantee that they would be absorbed into the
hearts and minds of white Americans. Historically, America has
shown that it is quite difficult to order or decree moral decency
and universal humanity on all of its citizens. The possibility that
race neutrality can effectively penetrate the American psyche en
masse is a rhetorical exercise at best.

THE BACKLASH

The backlash to social programs and federally sponsored
measures to level the playing field for African Americans speaks
volumes in this regard. The backlash is evident in America's
social-political shift backward to radical conservative ideas and
political platforms of the pre-civil rights period. One of the ways
that the quality-of-life disparities between Blacks and whites is

maintained is through color-blind ideology as Gabriel (1998) states, "In all its political guises, whiteness shares a point of privilege, a position of power from which it has been possible to define, regulate, judge as well as accrue material and symbolic rewards" (p. 184).

The color-blind argument is dependent upon and situated in the power of white American privilege; which means that they can give the illusion of it, grant it, or refuse it. Once again African Americans are forced to be dependent upon individuals whose interests are served by adhering to the color-blind position Gutmann (1995) asserts:

> Those of us who have unfairly benefited in the past, or will unfairly benefit in the future, if we do not act to change things, have special obligations, which flow from the general obligation to do our fair share to help others. We have these special obligations not because we asked to be unfairly advantaged, but because we have been and are unfairly advantaged. Because being white and affluent has been a source of unfair benefits in this country, fairness generates special obligations that are color-and class-conscious. (p. 342)

Gutmann makes the point that it is the obligation of whites to address the inequalities that exist between Blacks and whites in America because of unearned white privilege. This obligation is a responsibility that in the current social-political climate few white Americans appear to acknowledge or accept at the collective level. The word color-blind has favorable emotive properties (Rotunda, 1986) but its actual political operations are not so innocent. The color-blind position is located inside of a rhetorical mask that is used to obscure its larger meanings. Ani (1994) refers to this as "rhetorical ethic":

> The European rhetorical ethic is precisely that— purely rhetorical—and, as such, has its own origins as a creation for export; i.e., for the political, intercultural activity of the European. It is designed to create

an image that will prevent others from successfully anticipating European behavior, and its objective is to encourage nonstrategic (i.e., naïve, rather than successful) political behavior on the part of others. (This is the same as "nonpolitical" behavior.) It is designed to sell, to dupe, to promote European nationalistic objectives. It "packages" European cultural imperialism in a wrapping that makes it appear more attractive, less harmful. None of these features represents what can culturally be referred to as an "ideal" in any sense" (p. 316)

Color-blind ideology is currently being propagated to continue a backlash against the social programs left over from the Great Society of the 1960s. By using this term, neoliberals and conservatives can declare that America is color-blind without acknowledging or compensating for its racialized past, which has caused the current quality-of-life imbalances between most whites and many African Americans. The current political climate does not exist in a vacuum, but is reflective of the ideological desires from forces that oppose government-supported intervention with social programs. The virulent strains of anti-affirmative action, anti-immigration, and welfare programs suggest that the only version of color-blind positions that are acceptable are those that do not disrupt the current power dynamic that exists in America between whites and African Americans, as Herring and Amissah (1997) assert: "As a nation founded on the basis of Euro-centric images, the ethnocentric ideologies in force are those that purport the superiority of European cultural forms and promote the domination of non-whites or non-westerners"(p. 125). The prevailing neoliberal and conservative position admonishes African Americans to just get over it and move on, as Salins (1997) maintains:

In turn, blacks would do well to accept contemporary American disavowals of racism at face value; forgive American society for its legacy of injustice and discrimination; set aside any residue of anger and grievance, no matter how well justified; and let

bygones be bygones. No amount of anger and grievance can repair old wrongs; only holding America to
its founding ideals can do that. (p. 181)

Salins speaks to the reality that African Americans face in the
current social/political climate. African Americans are expected
in most quarters to accept the past, not challenge it, and at the
same time assume that America has transcended its racial past.
The color-blind argument lives inside of anti-egalitarian prerogatives as Fiske (1996) argues, "Whiteness is not an essence but a
power whose techniques differ according to the conditions of
its application. The most common can be cataloged, though,
not exhaustively, for new techniques will always be developed to
meet new conditions" (p. 42).

The color-blind position is based on a mythical optimism,
an optimism that is dependent on the good intentions of individuals who seem not to possess the political will to challenge
or change the existing social, political, and economic hierarchies
between Blacks and whites in America. The color-blind argument's placebo-like attachments obscure its distortions of reality.
The neutral tenets of the color-blind position have the potential
to manipulate African Americans into accepting the idea that
they have some control over this situation as Hanchard (2006)
maintains:

> One of the aspects of U.S. African American experi-
> ence that distinguished the black population from its
> white counterparts was its paradoxical location as a
> marginalized group within a powerful nation-state.
> This paradoxical location remains, I believe a key
> defining feature of U.S. African American political
> participation in deliberation and debate in society,
> civil society, and in more global, multinational public
> spheres. (p. 135)

The bizarre self assertive color-blind decree, "I don't believe
in race", by African Americans offers a tenuous sense of agency.
This agency is predicated on a naïve version of utopian speculation as A.N. Wilson (1993) observes:

> There are some "negroes" who seek to escape their
> history and identity by telling themselves, "I don't
> see color." Well, do you think that means the world
> doesn't see you as "colored"? A lot of people fail to
> understand that because they may choose not to see
> something in a certain way that other people still may
> choose to do so. (p. 38)

Looking at this reality in terms of implementation Hanchard
(2006) maintains:

> Neither black intellectuals nor black middle classes
> more generally are in positions of power and author-
> ity to determine how tax revenues are spent, which
> businesses move in or out of neighborhoods, and
> what infrastructures should be in place to improve
> the lives of black poor. (p. 142)

In the final analysis, it is up to coalitions of whites and Blacks to
change the hearts and minds of white lawmakers to demand that
the structures of America are in true alignment with the Constitution of the United States. Clearly, the color-blind argument
is mere manipulation of African Americans, as Schiller (1973)
explains:

> For manipulation to be most effective, evidence of its
> presence should be nonexistent. When the manipu-
> lated believe things are the way they are naturally
> and inevitably, manipulation is successful. In short
> manipulation requires a false reality that is a continu-
> ous denial of its existence. It is essential, therefore,
> that people who are manipulated believe in the neu-
> trality of their key institutions. (p. 11)

The experience of African Americans in America has been
a constant struggle to avail themselves of the neutrality inherent in the fundamental precepts found in the Constitution,
the Declaration of Independence, and the Bill of Rights. These
struggles have been waged since the forced placement of Africans

in Jamestown in 1619 and the battle continues. The historical record does not demonstrate that anti-egalitarian white Americans have an interest in the color-blind idea other than to serve their material and political interests; nor is it recorded that they will sacrifice their unearned privilege to actualize it for African Americans. The vast majority of whites appear to be attracted to the "pretense" of a color-blind society only when its serves their social, political, and economic interests. This position is based on an observation of a formula that is inherent in the color-blind argument. The formula is advanced by Derrick Bell (2004) and is as follows: "Justice for blacks vs. racism = racism" and "Racism vs. obvious perceptions of white self-interest = justice for blacks" (p. 50). Bell exposes the color-blind position because he brings to the surface the idea that unless whites benefit from policy changes in addition to Blacks, the changes will not take place. Bell examines this reality further in his "Interest –Convergence Principle", where he argues the principle has two rules:

> Rule1. The interest of blacks in achieving racial equality will be accommodated only when that interest converges with the interests of whites in policy-making positions. This convergence is far more important for gaining relief than the degree of harm suffered by blacks or the character of proof offered to prove harm. Rule 2. Even when interest-convergence results in an effective racial remedy, that remedy will be abrogated at the point that policymakers fear the remedial policy is threatening the superior societal status of whites, particularly those in the middle and upper classes. (p. 69)

Color-blind ideology serves the interests of domination by its false implication that the human principles of equality and race-neutrality are inherent in its mission, which was originally advanced in the Constitution. These two notions are separate and distinct for African Americans. The African American has the double burden of, first, being accepted as an equal, and second, having that equality legally inscribed into the structural operations of American life by individuals who may not view

African Americans as equals. Domination has shifted its formations from the old coercive state-endorsed physical models of the
American South to new amorphous varieties that have emerged
to take the place of the successful but outdated archetypes of
American domination. Winant (2001) observes, "This new
system can maintain white supremacy better than the old one.
This system of racial hegemony can present itself as color-blind
and multicultural..." (p. 309). Winant speaks to a reality that
few color-blind proponents want to engage. The issues that this
idea seeks to ignore will not disappear by the mere declaration of
color-blindness.

The continued disparities in the quality-of-life between
Blacks and whites illuminate the structural and political empti-
ness of the color-blind idea. The material conditions and realities
of race is a crucial element missing from the color-blind position
as Powell (2007) contends:

> Black unemployment is more than twice the white
> rate—a wider gap than in 1972. This means that one
> in nine African Americans cannot find a job. In terms
> of home ownership, the rate for whites has jumped
> from 65 percent to 75 percent since 1970. Black
> home ownership has only risen from 42 percent to
> 48 percent. At this rate, it would take approximately
> 1,660 years to close the home ownership gap, which
> amounts to about fifty-five generations. Health
> disparities also persist. Black infants are almost
> two-and-a-half times as likely as white infants to die
> before age one—a greater gap than in 1970. (p. 42)

This color-blind argument has no recognizable investment in
addressing the disparate outcomes in the lives of blacks and
whites unless it errs on the side of whites and inequality.

In terms of national ideology the American people receives
many of its cues from government-related activities in the public
sphere. The tone of American government sends a message to
Americans citizens and that is reflected in their attitudes toward
each other to some degree. Color-blind ideology is not above
this reality. According to Neville et al. (2005), there is emerg-

ing research on the color-blind position and levels of prejudice. Neville, Lilly, Duran, Lee and Browne (2000, pp. 59-70) report that among a mostly white sample, the level and amount of endorsement of the color-blind position was related to increased:

(1) Racial and gender intolerance,
(2) Racism against blacks, and
(3) Belief in a just world.

Critiques of the color-blind position have been noted by other scholars as Neville et al. (2005) maintain:

> Attending to these social realities, scholars have interjected a structural component to the term. Social scientists argue that a color-blind racial framework is a contemporary set of beliefs that serves to minimize, ignore, and/or distort the existence of race and racism; at its core is the belief that racism is a thing of the past and that race and racism do not play an important role in current social and economic realities (e.g., Bonilla-Silva, 2001, 2003; Carr, 1997) (p. 29).

The color-blind argument, if accepted uncritically by African Americans, has the potential to disrupt, neutralize, and reduce the efforts of African Americans to engage in their ancestral right to challenge the inequities that exist in American society. Color-blindness for many whites in America continues to legitimize racism, with the end result being the protection of their group interests by perpetuating and maintaining their racial privileges (Neville et al. 2005). There are dangers for African Americans engaging in uncritical acceptance of color-blind ideology. Scholars have suggested a possible connection between adoption of a color-blind racial framework and its relationship to working against one's group interest, specifically for African Americans (Neville, Worthington & Spanierman, 2001).

Uncritical acceptance of the color-blind racial framework by African Americans may lead to what Jost and Benaji (1994) termed "false consciousness", which they argue is, "...the holding of beliefs that are contrary to one's personal or group interest and which thereby contribute to the maintenance of the disadvantaged position of the self or the group" (p. 3). In amplification of Jost and Banaji's (1994) position, Neville et al. (2005) argue:

> In essence, false consciousness reflects an internalized, culturally sanctioned belief that encourages individuals in a stratified society to adopt the view point of those in power. Acceptance of the dominant viewpoint, in turn serves to keep minorities in a subjugated position by justifying their oppression and thus encouraging inertia. (p. 31)

Monocultural hegemony is the engine that drives the colorblind position. Hidden inside of its benevolent claims is a superstructure, which is dependent upon the maintenance of the European American norm as the standard for ideas and behavior for all members of the human family to be judged. African Americans who completely absorb this standard are rewarded in American society because of their wholesale acceptance of the European American norm. African Americans who adopt ideas that do not serve their collective and communal interests are bound to be contributors to their own oppression and ineffective agents in the struggle for African American agency. It is this reality that places the color-blind argument in alignment with ideologies and actions that have sought to silence the self-determinative instincts of people of African descent in America.

The presumed objectivity of the color-blind position leaves the definition of itself to those who wield power. As Asante (1990) asserts, "I have argued that what passes for objectivity is a sort of European subjectivity. Therefore, it may not serve any useful purpose to speak of objectivity and subjectivity as this division is artificial in and of itself" (p. 25). The noble idea that "American Democracy is color-blind" (Killian, 1968, p. 8), suffers from the recalcitrance of some whites in their inability to grant equal status to Blacks. According to Hacker (1992), "But white Americans, who both grant and impose racial memberships, show little inclination toward giving full nationality to the descendants of African slaves" (p. 17). The individualism and competitive nature of American society will continue to prevent equality between Blacks and whites. Winant (2004) asserts, "Yet in racial terms democracy remains precarious. Race-conscious democracy has never been realized" (p. 38). The idea that a move forward for Blacks is a move backward for whites is still salient in American life. Many white Americans appear to support notions about sameness or color-blindness yet they also support ideas and opinions that seek to prove how different African Americans are. As Hacker (1992) observes:

> ...William Shockley, a winner of the Nobel Prize, who argued that evidence showed people of African origin to be lower on an evolutionary scale. Another well known name is Arthur Jensen, a professor of psychology at the University of California. His stated position has been that because black children are genetically inferior, even compensatory programs like Head Start will fail because the native talents are not there. (p. 30)

The publishing, motivations, and funding schemes of these types of academic endeavors heighten the tensions that exist between Blacks and whites. This limits meaningful dialogues concerning the civic virtues of a just egalitarianism in American society. The unintended or intended consequences of this type of scholarship lead to reactionary public policies that erode the positive possibility of the color-blind project. The research and opinions expressed by conservative social scientists do not go unnoticed by white Americans because of their amplification by academic think tanks and media instruments. These positions can be identified as defenses for racialized cutbacks in government programs, as well as to set the social political climate for backlash. African American demands to redress the historical imbalance that exists because of decades of state-sanctioned structural inequities between Blacks and whites are seen by many whites as calls for entitlements that they believe are the cause of the problems in the first place.

Absent from the discourse concerning the color-blind argument is the discussion of structurally entrenched power. Power is the defining element that will allow or disallow the basic tenets of the color-blind argument to have substance in the institutions of America. A.N. Wilson (1998) posits:

> Power may conceivably refer to the ability to achieve a desired goal, or to the ability to willfully resist or overcome certain social and environmental conditions imposed on oneself by others, or the ability to impose on others against their will or outside their awareness, certain social, environmental circumstances and behavioral demands. (p. 8)

Power will determine how color-blind ideology actually is framed and formed in the public sphere. Entrenched structural power that is housed in the legislative, judicial, and executive branches of the federal government has shown little interest in the versions of color-blindness that are concerned with restructuring relationships of power between Blacks and whites, as Haney Lopez (2006) asserts: "...its greatest potency instead lies in preserving the racial status quo" (p. 158). The color-blind position does not acknowledge the continued power of racism in America but argues that racism is a thing of the past. Speaking to neoconservatism and the racial project Omi and Winant (1994) observe, "It sketched out a vision of an "egalitarian" society where racial considerations were no longer the concern of state policy" (p. 118). Color-blind proponents present contemporary America as a place free from lasting racial division (Haney Lopez, 2006). This allows their argument to go forward with empty slogans and phrases that have no basis in the racial realities of the United States. Developing in America is a new kind of hierarchy, which Haney Lopez (2006) calls "Color-blind White dominance" (pp. 147-148). He contends:

> This looming racial paradigm has three central elements: 1) continued racial dominance by whites; 2) an expansion of who counts as white along socio-racial rather than bio-racial lines; and (3) a

color-blind ideology that simultaneously proclaims a robust commitment to antiracism yet works assiduously to prevent effective remediation. (p.148)

Haney Lopez illuminates the central meanings of the color-blind position that are problematic for African Americans. Color-blind ideology represents the changing face of domination in America. Steinberg (1995) contends:

> For the color-blind right *culture* is the key factor in explaining the underclass. For the "color-blind left," it is class—which is to say, the economic factors that keep people trapped in poverty. What these positions have in common is a neglect of *race* –that is, the specifically racist structures that keep racial minorities trapped in poverty. (p. 140)

Realizing little currency in the biologically determined ideas of subjugation, domination now seeks to rearticulate inequities and oppression (Omi and Winant, 1994). The suggestion that the liberal state is responsible for reverse racist preferential treatment of Blacks and other people of color gives the color-blind argument a platform to argue for race-neutral policies.

Color-blind ideology urges the state to remove itself from the process of redressing the historical imbalances in quality-of-life that exist between whites and Blacks. As Sears, Hetts, Sidanius, and Bobo (2000) observe, "Almost all whites support general principles of equal treatment, but are more divided about government action to ensure it, and most oppose race-conscious policies, such as preferential treatment" (p. 33). The energy against so-called preferential treatment is suggestive of an anti-egalitarian doctrine that is subsumed inside of the color-blind position and made possible because of whites control of power apparatuses, as Samuel Huntington (2003) argues:

> ...power is the ability of one person or group to change the behavior of another person or group. Behavior may be changed through inducement, coercion, or exhortation, which require the power-

wielder to have economic, military, institutional, demographic, political, technical, social, or other resources. The power of a state or group is hence normally estimated by measuring the resources it has at its disposal against those of the other states or groups it is trying to influence. (pp. 83-84)

America has at its disposal all of the elements described by Huntington to make color-blindness an institutional reality. What America does not appear to possess is the humanistic or collective political will to do so. In order for the colorblind-argument to be just and egalitarian it must demand that American institutions acknowledge the imbalances of the past in substantive terms and not continue to rely on hollow phrases when they are politically expedient. The color-blind idea must provide, along with financially able blacks, ameliorative solutions to the problems that continue to plague African Americans such as: education, job training, health care, and housing just to name a few.

The neoliberal and conservative social climate present at this time in America has shown little interest in reinvigorating the aforementioned realities. Resistance to these ideas exists in the highest judicial branch of American government as well as the hearts of the common man, which in turn exposes the nature and futility of the color-blind project. Consequently, color-blind ideology contributes to the maintenance of the asymmetrical social, political, and economic disparities that exist between most Blacks and many whites in America.

Chapter 4

THE POST-RACIAL PROJECT AND AFRICAN AMERICANS

In the aftermath of two terms of the Reagan presidency, the Republican Revolution, Contract with America, and the rise of "centrist" Democratic leadership, a surprising mix of intellectual, social, and political ideas emerged in the last decade of the 20th century to form the corpus of ideas located in the *Post-Racial Project*. Intellectual and political positions such as postmodernism, essentialism, the social construction of race argument, and color-blind ideology resulted in an amalgamation of discourses that have been employed to neutralize challenges to racial equity. These ideas have been aggressively rooted in methods of intellectual inquiry, scholarly debates, national conversation, policy speak, and the cultural landscape on many levels. The illumination, exploration, and critique of the post-racial discursive interventions present in this body of ideas is critical because if accepted uncritically these concepts have the potential to reduce the collective agency of African Americans.

In order to do investigate so-called post racialism it is important to examine public discourse. The role of public discourse and the creation of a discursive community is vital to understanding ideological domination and its influences on African Americans.

Discursive communities set the climate for the acceptance of ideologies as Fiske (1996) maintains:

> Discourse, then is always a terrain of struggle, but the struggle is never conducted on a level field. The dominant discourses, those that occupy the mainstream, serve dominant interests, for they are products of the history that has secured their domination. (p. 5)

This chapter will explore the significance of these ideas as well as investigate their current meanings on the lives of African Americans. This investigation is warranted because as Fiske argues, "We use discourse, then, both to form our sense of the social world and to form the relations by which we engage in it" (p. 6).

Understanding the contemporary influence of ideological domination on the lives of African Americans and its continued influence on this population's historical quest for self-determination and agency is vital in the 21st century. While racism, prejudice, bigotry, and discrimination have become familiar terms in the lexicon of America's social vocabulary, ideological domination remains in large measure mis-understood, particulary in terms of public discourse and its unique ability to shape ideas and influence public opinion.

IDEOLOGICAL THREATS TO AFRICAN AMERICANS

This section examines what I have determined are *contemporary ideological threats to the internal security of African Americans.* The first ideological threat that I have identified is the Post-Racial Project, which I define as: ideas in modern thought such as postmodernism, color blindness, essentialism, the social construction of race, and the corollary assumptions located in victim blame and so-called race-neutral discourses. These areas range from politics to cinema, but the most protracted and robust forms of the Post-Racial Project can be observed in discourse surrounding institutional reforms such as affirmative action, welfare reform, higher education admission policies, judicial decisions, and hiring practices. The specific focus of this work is centered upon an illumination of how the ideas and positions located in the Post-Racial Project are being used as the principal arguments by individuals and groups determined to create legislative and policy mandates to end race-based initiatives in all spheres of public life. What I felt was warranted by an *African-centered theorist* is a captious investigation, which seeks to demonstrate how ideological domination remains an obstacle for most African Americans and how this population's collective spirit of resistance may be neutralized by the uncritical acceptance of the corpus of ideas located in the Post-Racial Project.

The hegemonic political nature of these ideologies and their dangers to the collective agency of African Americans become clear when the implications of the four pillars of the Post-Racial Project are examined.

POSTMODERNISM
- Against theory and methodology
- Nothing is to be accepted or rejected, no universal truths or objective knowledge
- Reality and human events are fluid and beyond measurement

ESSENTIALISM
- A proposition stating that certain characteristics possessed by a group are universal, and not dependent on circumstances or historical situations
- Rejection of a bonded cultural essence among human groups

COLOR BLINDNESS
- Race should not be taken into consideration when trying to address racial equity
- Opposes race based remedial programs at the federal, state and local levels

SOCIAL CONSTRUCTION OF RACE
- Suppresses, minimizes, and/ or ignores the material consequences of a racialized world

As a dominative ideology, the Post-Racial Project that is currently embedded in public discourse has the potential to set a climate of nonresistance among African Americans. This collection of ideas, if accepted uncritically, may lead to a collective psychosocial and political passivity, which in effect will allow the entrenched existing inequality to continue unabated. In order to expose the hegemonic nature of the Post-Racial Project and its influence on public discourse, two realities must be identified: (1) The role of public discourse and (2) the creation of a discursive community. Clarity about this symbiotic relationship is vital to understanding ideological domination and its influences on African Americans. It is important for all free- thinking individuals to understand and remember that discursive communities set the climate for the acceptance of ideologies.

After analyzing the major literature of the Post-Racial Project, I discovered a common philosophical thread that drove me to four major assumptions. The Post-Racial Project is:

1. Anti-foundational
2. Against identity formations
3. Anti-group based social and cultural cohesive structuring
4. Against any form of grand narrative

This is illuminating because as human beings we use discourse to give us a sense of social reality. After careful review and critical analysis, what I was able to uncover about the central tenets of the Post-Racial Project is that by utilizing the "essentialist" position, which is against any sense of collective racial identity formations, African Americans are disproportionately singled out and critiqued as the group that could benefit the most by abandoning their African cultural foundations and historically rooted traditions and practices. I locate the Post-Racial Project as an anti-egalitarian non-African paradigm. In my view as an African-centered theorist, developing a conceptual counter argument to the Post-Racial Project was a task of immediate urgency. I now restate for emphasis as noted earlier in this work the definition and operationalization of the conceptual counter argument that I term Agency Reduction Formation or (ARF). An Agency Reduction Formation is any system of thought that distracts, neutralizes, or reduces the need and desire for assertive collective agency by African Americans.

The ARF concept is useful because it gives individuals concerned about racial equity, social justice, and human rights a definitive conceptual counter argument that exposes the dominative nature and hegemonic frameworks located in the Post-Racial Project, which, if accepted uncritically *ultimately* is the suppression of African American agency. Clearly, in order to have a theoretical understanding of agency we must be grounded in the three primary spheres that comprise African agency: group autonomy, collective self-determination, and communal sovereignty. The central danger of the Post-Racial Project is its rhetoric, which does not match established empirical realities. The ideas located in the Post-Racial Project do not reflect the structural, institutional, and systemic lived realities of most African Americans. There is a lack of continuity between the Post-Racial Project's public pronouncements through its rhetoric and central ideas versus the daily lives of many African Americans. The difference between the two realities is striking because the rhetoric does not deliver where it matters most, in the quality-of-life indicators. Consequently, there is a glaring disconnect when we look at the major quality-of-life and social indicators such as jobs, income, unemployment, housing, health care, and education, because the Post-Racial Project does not empirically demonstrate an honest or transparent connection between its enduring contradictions. Its central ideas encourage African Americans to see little value in advancing race-based identities and racialized realties, which is problematic specifically when investigating material outcomes that we can examine at the structural, institutional, and systemic level. According to Powell (2007):

> In 1968, the typical black family had 60 percent as much income as a white family. Today it has only 58 percent as much. In 1968, for every dollar of white per capita income, African Americans earned fifty-five cents. Today they earn only fifty-seven cents. At

this pace, it would take blacks 580 years to make up
the remaining forty-three cents. Similarly, at the slow
rate that the black white poverty gap has been nar-
rowing since 1968, it would take approximately 150
years to close. (p. 42)

The empirical realities of the major social indicators do not
match the rhetoric of the Post-Racial Project on any level.

The abysmal disparities between African Americans and
whites are consistent no matter which quality-of-life or social
indicator one investigates, be it education, health care, housing,
and the ones I previously mentioned, the situation is clear. Also,
it does not matter where one examines the data, whether it is the
Census Bureau, Government Accounting Office, Bureau of Labor
Statistics, or left-leaning or right-wing think tanks, the statistical
realities are asymmetrical in relation to the rhetoric of the Post-
Racial Project. African Americans have not caught up nor is this
population as a group catching up at the rate of others in terms
of the major quality-of-life indicators. The Post-Racial Project
does not identify or acknowledge these disparities because its
central tenets see little value in communal, collective identity
formations for African Americans. Therefore, I advance the idea
that when these very nuanced but subversive articles of bad faith
located in the Post-Racial Project go unchallenged, a deracination
process could develop that may produce in African Americans,
both adults and children, a national behavior and psychological
infrastructure that is "resistant to resistance." This is important
when we are looking at the healthy African mind. According
to the leading research and most-cited literature in the field of
African-centered psychology, the healthy African mind is committed to a strong collective African survival thrust, as well as an
un-yielding, un-wavering spirit of race maintenance (Sutherland,
1997; Wilson, 1999). Clearly, this work does not speak to the
unhealthy African mind, which is dislocated and needs African-
centered cognitive behavioral therapy along with various forms of
relocation interventions and re-centering. I want to be clear and
emphatically suggest that this work is geared toward the healthy
African mind, not those Africans who willingly and willfully

engage in and submit to consensual domination. This work is an African-centered, forward thinking project on all levels.

We have seen this type of ideology before but this time it is hiding in the Post-Racial Project in the 21st century. Therefore, I locate the Post-Racial Project as *the third stage of the seasoning process.* The first stage took place in the 17th century in the agrarian plantation structures of the Caribbean Basin and North America when captive Africans were forced to abandon their African cultures, traditions, customs, values, folkways, mores, languages, and even their ideas of God. The second stage was the development of the Black patriot. This is the 20th century Post-World War II American notion of rewarding the compliant African American for his ideological dependability and cultural congruency. The third stage of the seasoning process consists of the 21st century *Post-Racial Agency Reduction Formations* found in the Post-Racial Project which have already been introduced. I am advancing the idea that all three of the aforementioned seasoning stages contain a similar goal: To set the climate for the abandonment and disengagement of Africans in America from race- specific strategies and initiatives in public life that lead to race maintenance, survival thrust, and ultimately to collective agency for African people.

A long-range analysis suggests that an uncritical acceptance of the Post-Racial Project may lead to a re-marginalization of African Americans without a clearly recognizable anti-egalitarian footprint because of the hidden and unclear meanings of the tropes positioned in the ideologies of the Post-Racial Project. In retrospect, I remain empathetic to Dr. Martin Luther King's prophetic call when he said on August 28, 1963 "I have a dream my four children will one day live in a nation where they will not be judged by the color of their skin but by the content of their character." However, until that prophetic statement is reflected in the structural, institutional, systemic, and material realities for African Americans en masse, this is not the time for African Americans to lay down our guard, abandon Dr. King's dream, and allow the predatory collection of ideas located in the Post-Racial Project's mythical optimism and utopian speculation to guide our thinking about reality. Nor should we allow our children to fall prey to Walt Disney-esque fantasy and surreal ideas about human activity and social relations. The Post-Racial Project's creation of a Potemkin village of double dialectics and nuanced escapes from structural, institutional, and systemic realities must be challenged wherever it lives in the lives of African people. For the record, I have heard and read the proponents of the Post-Racial Project attempt to make this a generational issue by arguing that this generation has not experienced racism like the civil rights generation, but quite frankly I submit that because you have not had attack dogs and fire hoses put upon your person does not give you the right to ignore collective Black suffering, nor does it give one license to abandon one's ancestral responsibility to support and engage in agency-producing activities that uplift and advance African people in the first decade of the 21st century.

The ideologies located in the Post-Racial Project must not be allowed to run amok, without an African-centered analysis that is invested in and amplifies the communal benefits of collective agency-driven racial orientations. Aggressive forms of Agency Reduction Formations such as postmodernism, color-blind ideology, essentialism, and the social construction of race argument are suppressive ideological tools that, if misunderstood by African Americans, may contribute to this populations continued marginalization. Agency Reduction Formations disrupt the human harmony that is possible when all members of the human family are allowed honest efforts at their own group agency. The following considerations will propel and leverage this work into the public sphere where it can be used to stand against the articles of bad faith and subversive elements located in the Post-Racial Project.

CONSIDERATIONS

- Confront and engage the Post-Racial Project with the empirical and statistical realities of African Americans.
- Understand that the collection of ideologies located in the Post-Racial Project suppress African American agency.
- Maintain vigilance and defeat legislative initiatives on all levels that reflect the prerogatives of the Post-Racial Project.

This work acts as a sentinel, a clarion call to individuals who refuse to allow the anti-egalitarian ideological elements of the Post-Racial Project to remain aloft and unchallenged in the arena of social justice and equality. These ideologies are not transcending or transformative but cleverly veiled dispositions cloaked in seductive, agency-reducing positions that masquerade as benign humanistic ideas, but at their core is a malignant set of principles set out to distract African Americans from the structural and empirical real-life disparities that are present and measurable in the major quality-of-life indicators. It is important that individuals concerned about social justice have a concrete understanding of the ideological architecture of the Post-Racial Project. It has the potential if left unchecked and without critical investigation of its inherent discourses to further distance from public consciousness the unique history of African Americans and their documented relationship to racial and social injustice in the American context. Clearly, an uncritical wholesale acceptance of the Post-Racial Project as it currently stands against established empirical and statistical reality is counterintuitive, and not in the best interests of African Americans.

VICTIM BLAME IDEOLOGY AND AFRICAN AMERICANS

An emerging new form of old sentiments reformulated as anti-Black responses was given birth just before, during and after the Contract with America phase of American politics. These forms of discourse seek to silence challenges to historical imbalances, suppress dissent, neutralize political opposition, and summarily deny African Americans the right to redress the quality-of-life disparities that exist in America. Housed inside of the rhetoric of the *victim blame* position (Ryan, 1971) is the denial of African American voices that challenge the status quo in the United States. The victim blamers seek to silence voices of opposition. Positions that expose, or argue against dominative privilege are summarily dismissed by victim blame proponents as eager manipulations by African Americans seeking a "handout."

Using the arguments of conservative behavioralists, this idea casts full responsibility back onto African Americans for their lack of agency on all levels of life. Backlash from white Americans resulted in new forms of social, political, and economic philosophies directed toward the continued maintenance of privilege and power in America. Following the lead of the contemporary conservative rise to power, victim blame ideology developed new articulations of racialized meanings ascribed to various connotations of self-help, personal responsibility, and agency for African Americans. Singularly choosing the African American experience in America as the model for reprobation, the positions taken by journalists, academics, policy analysts, think tanks, policymakers, as well as the rank and file sought to promulgate this group as society's social pathogens with the only conceivable fix being "tough love", that is, abandonment. Growing tired and anxious from what they viewed as decades of abuses of the system, reactionary conservatives designed rhetorical campaigns with the intent to build public interest and set the climate for political support directed toward an attack on the African American poor.

The hands-off laissez-faire policies that are touted as helping the Black poor absolve whites of their role in the creation of inequality and give wealthy Blacks an excuse from using their economic clout to change the conditions that most African Americans are forced to contend with in their daily lives. Victim blaming is a different type of invisible Jim Crow. Victim blame ideology serves as a form of cognitive therapy for the privileged because it distorts the language while altering the perspectives used surrounding suffering and collective responsibility (Cole, 2007). In victim blame ideology the term "victim" is used as a derisive description by the adherents of this ideology. According to Cole:

> The most salient common element shared by these writers, by contrast with most previous uses of the term "victim", is that they employ it pejoratively. "Victim" is deployed to dismiss, ridicule, and condemn rather than to evoke sympathy, empathy or even pity. Individuals and groups who claim to have been victimized are portrayed as weak, manipulative, self-indulgent, helpless, hopeless dependents. (p. 22)

The portrayals that are a common thread of victim blame ideology afford the blamers a measure of relief, distance, and a sanctimonious platform to argue against their human responsibility to offer understanding and possible aid to people who are less fortunate than them. Contentious and absent of empirical support, the anecdotal diatribes they advance are located in texts such as: (Dershowitz, 1994; D'Souza, 1991; Elder, 2000; Hughes, 1993; McWhorter, 2000; and Sykes, 1992) which espouse the painful but as they see it deserving position of poor Blacks. The victim blame proponents believe the circumstances of poor Blacks are totally of their own doing and give no voice to the possibility that structural forces could affect the blamed.

The backdrop that victim blame ideology operates from is dependent upon a political climate that rewards so-called winners and punishes what it deems as losers, specifically when they are Black. As is the case with most radical conservative race-based arguments; the past is treated ahistorically. The past is a historical footnote serving only to remind the victim blamers of their ancestors' glory and struggle but never is it used to understand current disparities between whites and Blacks in America. Victim blame ideology is not the singular domain of white academics. There is a rapidly growing cadre of well-paid Black scholars and pundits who are deeply invested in the lucrative utility of the ahistorical view of history as well. Taking the position of "helping" their brethren, these individuals brandish harsh criticism for what they have been told and led to believe are African Americans' culturally based pathological natures. In many cases they are rewarded with handsome supplemental incomes from neoliberal and conservative think tanks, who procure for them access to the major media outlets so they can assume their anointed role as sirens of truth in a world full of quiet anguish. McWhorter (2000) writes, "In that light, I believe that the black community today is the main obstacle to achieving the full integration our Civil Rights leaders sought" (p. x). Alternatively, Hilliard (1998) asserts, "These Europeans are particularly pleased with confused Africans who see themselves as allied with no ethnic group – "just people"—because it provides evidence that they will support white supremacy" (p.39).

The victim blame position absolves its proponents of any responsibility to address what many scholars (Asante, 2003b; Hacker, 1992; Kovel, 1984; Massey& Denton, 1993; Neubeck &Cazenave, 2001; Omi & Winant, 1994; Sears, Hetts, Sidanius, & Bobo, 2000; Sutherland, 1997; and W.D. Wright, 1998) agree is a major roadblock to American progress and that is American racism. McWhorter's assessment is akin to the impossibility of Black people operating in a world without white influences as Kovel (1984) contends:

> In any case, for the black individual there is no escaping the whiteness of the society except by denying who he or she is—and that is no escape at all. It does not matter if he makes a million dollars a year for leaping high above a ten-foot basket; or accumulates many more millions by selling records; or constitutes a technical-professional elite in a city like Atlanta; or even gets to sit on the board of directors of truly white corporations, or in the Cabinet or the Supreme Court—he, or she, will still be defined by an order whose power and dominion are white. And in this order, blackness is Otherness. There is no escaping this, just as there is no escaping language. (p. xxxviii)

The bulk of McWhorter's arguments are based upon personal observations bereft of detailed research of historical or contemporary events, empirical reality, and research methods. McWhorter even abandons his academic training in linguistics for more polemical stances. McWhorter (2000) holds, "Whites also unwittingly encourage all of these currents via well-intentioned social policies like open-ended welfare and permanent affirmative action, which are intended to help blacks overcome..." (p. xiii). To the critical observer this statement conveys that McWhorter is unaware of the structural changes in welfare reform that were signed into law by President Clinton in1996. It seems implausible that a person who is in the employ of a major conservative think tank such as the Manhattan Institute and compensated to critique national (Black) ideas would not be aware of public information—unless McWhorter is intentionally misleading his readers with his rants.

Purposefully placed misleading terms like "open-ended" and "permanent" are agenda-based, ideological slogans deployed to insure the perpetuation of conflict between Blacks and whites.

This type of scholarship in some cases emanates from individuals who are not empirically trained in the social sciences, so therefore they are incapable of bringing forth sound data to support their arguments and positions as Cole (2007) asserts, "Polemical in tone and based mostly on anecdotal data, conceptual rigor is not one of their stronger features" (p. 21). Victim blame ideology sets the climate for the rejection of altruistic remedies and leads to the continued unequal distribution of wealth and resources between Blacks and whites. This biased information eventually over time shifts Americans' humanistic sensibilities and creates resistance to the idea of aiding their fellow Americans. The victim blame argument focuses on the effects of the Black poor in terms of behavior and culture but does not consider the causal relationships of structural inequality. By focusing on the faults of those in need rather than the cause of their needs, this ideology effectively relieves its proponents of any responsibility. McNamee & Miller (2004) speak to this point:

> As long as people believe an ideology to be "true" then it is "true" for them in its consequences. People do not act on the world as it is but as they perceive and make sense of it. For ideologies of inequality to "legitimize" particular social arrangements, it is not necessary that the ideology be objectively true or even falsifiable; what matters is that people accept and act on it. (p. 3)

Creating a fault line and validating the natural white order is a vital mission of scholarship involved in the victim blame project. Black expositors of victim blame ideology (Carter, 1991; Keyes, 1995; Sowell, 2005; W.E. Williams, 1987; and Wortham, 1981) and others involved in this campaign give voice and validation to the racialized meaning of its central ideas and serve as a barrier to the charge of racism that may be hurled at white proponents. Additionally, a body of literature written by African Americans (Connerly, 2000; Elder, 2000; Steele, 1990; A. Williams, 1995;

and J.Williams, 2006) has emerged that further emboldens the victim blame rhetoric that is heard in the public sphere. Anecdotal notions of cultural pathology, dependency syndromes, and polemical catchphrases abound in the works of these writers, which increases white backlash sentiments and softens the blow of government reforms that are purely based on political dogma and conservative ideology.

Unfortunate circumstances occur in the lives of many white Americans from the Appalachian millwright to the factory worker of the Mississippi Delta. Why the unpredictable circumstances of poor and rich whites are not meted out in the same type of negative scholarly attentions is a matter of point. Lind (1996) writes:

> This explains, I think, why American public discourse is full of detailed discussions of the black underclass, while the subject of the white overclass hardly ever comes up—even though, in any objective account of America's troubles, the powerful and rich white overclass, not a small number of poor and violent ghetto residents, must be seen as playing the central role. (p. 140)

Victim blame ideology excoriates poor African Americas as if their economic challenges are completely of their own doing. This ideology rarely takes into account the structural changes in the U.S. economy and job market that came about as a result of corporate and government shifts (W.J. Wilson, 1987, 1996). The victim blame proponents rarely explore the residual effects of conditions that are unique to African Americans, such as American enslavement of Africans, Jim Crow, legal segregation, and contemporary racism. The victim blamers are shy to examine the historical conditions that produced the realities that many poor Blacks must face. This omission is a curious inconsistency that has not gone un-noticed by scholars. Delgado (1996) examines this:

> Law-and order conservatives want to deny any social obligation from the racist behavior of the early Colonials and Southern plantation owners. But they are happy to remind us that we owe obligations to

the document and nation that they set up. We owe obligations arising out of the social contract, but no obligation is owed to us arising from the abuse we suffered in connection with it. Ahistorical young conservatives want the benefit of social compliance from blacks with a system that provides young whites with security, schools, and liberty. But they don't want to pay for it by recognizing a debt they owe blacks arising from their forefather's wrongs. (p. 108)

It has yet to be empirically documented that a few decades of mild progress can undue 246 years of African enslavement or make up for 100 years of state-sanctioned unequal treatment of African Americans. The bias and lack of balance inherent in the examination of the historical record by victim blamers is telling and serves to illuminate the agenda attached to their project. In academic, political, and financial opportunity spheres, Black proponents of victim blame ideology benefit from their unrelenting cultural congruency and ideological dependability. Sutherland (1997) contends:

The Black elite has a long tradition of serving the interests of the oppressors and ignoring the common plight of Africans. They deny or reject the collective concerns of the African community and have invariably allied themselves with Europeans to obtain and preserve their short term personal gains." (p. 57)

Their steady and reliable adherence to conservative American ideals and wholesale uncritical acceptance of neoliberal and far right agendas make them valuable to the neoliberal neoconservative alliance on many levels. Black victim blamers' unique outlook on Black reality can be traced to dominative external stimuli. According to Harrell (1999), "In a similar fashion, the world created by white supremacy assaults the senses of African people with events and conditions. These circumstances cause one to engage in value judgments, evaluations, and attributions of causes" (p. 97). The uncritical stances on attribution and causality taken by many Black victim blamers is worthy of analysis. Harrell maintains:

However, the institutions of white supremacy craftily obscure certain portions of the contexts in which these events and conditions are embedded. Most people fail to identify the network of root causes that have brought these conditions into being. Robbed of an understanding of the network of causes, that is, of the full context surrounding these circumstances, African people will make fundamental errors in attributing causes. They will draw faulty conclusions and interpretations related to circumstances that surround the lives of many black people. These interpretations facilitate the development of mental structures that accommodate and reinforce white supremacy. (pp. 97-98)

Similarities exist between the liberal and conservative treatment of victim blame ideology as it suits their respective interests as they portray poor African Americans as a marginalized nation of mendicants. Both political parties support the capitalist system and have allegiance to the free marketplace. Liberals will at times allow government intervention for the oppressed as long as it does not interfere with commerce. Conservatives rarely advocate for government intervention for any reason, except corporate welfare, and believe the will of the state is most important, especially in issues surrounding race.

Consequently, as anti-egalitarian forces have shifted to some degree away from evolutionary racist dogma it has replaced this argument with victim blame ideology. Both ideas in their respective eras serve the distinct purpose of neutralizing meaningful conversations around racial bias, while subjugating and abandoning African Americans. The victim blame system maintains a system of privilege for most whites and compliant Blacks. If African Americans absorb these ideas into their choices for political office, legislative decisions, and other areas that involve their unique interests, they may be setting themselves up for continued domination. Conclusively, I maintain that victim blame ideology is an Agency Reduction Formation. As with all Agency Reduction Formations, their uncritical acceptance by African Americans leads to a collective destruction of the will to resist hegemonic practices, which serves to maintain the status quo ante and domination.

Chapter 5

THE MIS-DIRECTION OF THE CONTEMPORARY BLACK CHURCH

Spirituality played a vital role in the lives of African Americans in their indigenous homeland of Africa and continued after their forced relocation to the Americas. The enslavement period restricted and altered how Africans in America would worship and engage in the practice of faith. The rules of the enslavement period did not allow Africans in America to worship their indigenous Gods. Africans in America were forced to accept an alien version of spirituality, which held in its beliefs the idea that Africans were inferior to Europeans.

Over time this led to the development of a form of religious functioning that sought to address the needs of Blacks as Lincoln (1978) asserts:

> ...black religion in general, largely defined as a response to social construct which generally excludes black people from participation in the common values of the society, and which forces them to search for alternative compensatory values in mini-constructs of their own. (p. 8)

The notion of "alternative compensatory values" that Lincoln describes is problematic for African Americans. The abandonment of African spirituality by African Americans places them in a vulnerable position. The enslavement period led to the development of a religious base for African Americans that does not derive from their indigenous histories, cultural traditions, values, or cosmological ways of being. As Billingsley (1999) states, "More than one aspiring young black Christian has been prompted to ask: "Reverend, if we are made in the image of God, why is it that all the pictures of Jesus in our church show him as a white man?" (p.170). There are many layers to this dichotomy and its realities point to the central contradictions in the lives of African Americans who practice Christianity versus African spirituality. Azibo (2001) asserts:

> History is not just "dead dates", but a live component of the collective historical memory and one's extended-self concept. A people's history is inextricably linked to their identity. Whatever a group's historical contributions are are significant aspects of self-definition. Whenever religion is incongruous with African history, as defined, it harms African's historical memory and extended-self concept." (p. 98)

DEVELOPMENTS IN BLACK CHRISTIANITY

The focus of attention in this chapter is not to argue that one form of worship is superior to another, but to investigate if new developments in Black forms of Christianity best serve the needs and interests of African Americans or have they failed to advance them as a group. Black theologian James Cone gives a thorough going analysis of this question in his works: *A Black Theology of Liberation* (1970); *For My People* (1984); *Black Theology and Black Power* (1969); *Risks of Faith* (1999); *God of the Oppressed* (1975), and *Speaking the Truth* (1986). Cone's main contention is that unless Christianity fights for the liberation of the oppressed, it is not in the best interests of African Americans. W.R. Jones (1973) writes, "Cone declares: Either God is identified with the oppressed to the point that their experience becomes his, or he is a God of racism" (p. 72). The idea that a Christian God could be identified with oppression should give pause to African Americans' wholesale uncritical acceptance of it as their means to salvation. Azibo (2001) suggests that the acceptance of white Christianity without modifications by African Americans may lead to a form of psychological misorientation:

> Theological Misorientation is fundamentally defined by your author as the belief in, allegiance to, or practice of a theology, religion-related ideology or any aspects thereof that are incongruous with (a) Africentricity (as Black social theory), (b) African history, and (c) traditional African cosmology (e.g., harmony with nature, respect for and incorporation of the natural order inherent in the cosmos, spiritual and divine essence as the nature of the original human being, WEUSI, etc.). (p. 96)

The incongruity inherent in white Christianity and its complete adoption by African Americans, without modifications suited to their historical legacies, compromises its ability to advance the interests of Blacks in America and the world. As Azibo (2001) contends:

> ...all non-Africentric religions—especially those that purport explicit universality or those whose doctrines are determined by Arabs, Asian Indians, Gentile and Semite-Whites—serve to orient their African adherents (captives?) against African social theory and Self-maintenance and towards the sustentation of their own (non-African) group. (p. 97)

Contemporary Christianity, if it is to be useful for African Americans, must be altered to address the particular needs of African Americans as an oppressed people. The alterations must include the return to the affirmation of African spirituality and its precepts and a renewed focus on social justice issues affecting Black people in America. After African-centered modifications are instituted, contemporary Christianity can then be successfully utilized as a change agent for African Americans' disparate conditions in America as it has historically done. According to Swan (1981),

> The black church was the home of the birth of many national organizations and of the civil rights movement. It has become a most powerful institution because it is a definer of social norms and collective ideas and serves as a bulwark in the shared spiritual experiences of black people. The church has also been a force advocating economic, political, and social mobility for blacks. (p. 131)

This actuality places Christianity in its historical role of liberation instrument. African American religious practices must do more than just provide emotional comfort. Contemporary Christianity must provide energy for resistance against injustice and inequality directed toward Blacks. Because of the legacy of white supremacy and its appendages—such as racism, discrimination, prejudice, bigotry, and their resultant inequality—Black people must demand that their spiritual systems manifest in some form of agency production. Mays (1968) observes white Christianity this way, "...it has the tendency to lead one to take a complacent laissez-faire attitude toward life in that the person sees the will of God in all that happens" (pp. 71-72). God for African Americans should be more than a spiritual savior relieving one's guilt and delivering them from sin. God must be the liberator from oppression and white supremacy (Cone, 1975).

This is the distinction that must be made between Christianity for Blacks and whites. Whites in America do not experience racism from other whites as Blacks do, henceforth Blacks' respective interpretations and expectations of Christianity must be different in form and practice. If Blacks are to be Christians they must use Christianity as a divine force to fight inequality in the current social, political, and economic climate. Black Christians must harness the force that they believe exists in Christianity and call upon it to redress the existing imbalances in quality-of-life outcomes between Blacks and whites in the United States and the world. Cone (1975) asserts, "Salvation was not only a train and a ship but also a sweet chariot, swinging low, "coming for to carry me home" (p. 57). Christianity has a burden to bear for African Americans as Cone (1975) contends:

> It was the divine presence in their situation that held their humanity together in the midst of the brokenness of black existence. It was the power to endure in struggle and the patience to remain calm when surrounded by inexplicable evil. (p. 57)

THE WORD CHURCH

Contemporary Black Christianity in some quarters has abandoned its African roots and morphed into an alien spiritual culture. The most aggressive Agency Reduction Formation phenomenon in the contemporary Black church is the Word Church (Franklin, 1997). According to R.L. Smith (2007), "These churches proclaim a gospel message of health, wealth, and success through personal acts of heroic faith" (p. 146). Absorbing European cultural values, focusing on individualism, as well as espousing the attainment of wealth and its material trappings, this movement is a curious development for the African American church. Distancing itself from the virtues of the theology of the Civil Rights Movement, this brand of Black Christianity prides itself on values tied directly to American capitalism and European worldview. Social issues and legal reforms are not the main thrust of this movement. In most Word Churches economically challenged African Americans are left to fend for themselves in matters of public policy concerning health, education, employment, and civic participation— the bedrock issues lodged in the social reform theology that drove the Civil Rights Movement.

Caving into the American cultural exigencies of consumerism, materialism, and individualism the Word Churches seek to advance the notion that church is the place where African Americans can come and ask God to bless them with material well-being. Ideas such as challenging the status quo ante, protesting inequality, and other forms of dissent have taken a backseat to issues that involve the acquisition of wealth and material prosperity. Smith (2007) asserts:

> The content of their message tends to affirm and value the focus on individual faith and the ability of the individual to obtain and develop the means to increase material well-being. This is done often to the neglect of any serious focus on social issues such as sexism, racism, and class discrimination. (p. 147)

The traditional message of the Black church has historically been rooted in salvation and resistance against injustices perpetuated against African Americans. Burrow (2006) speaks to the legacy of Dr. Martin Luther King Jr.: "From his father and other black preachers, he learned that the God of the Hebrew prophets and Jesus worked cooperatively with humans to achieve the divine expectation that justice be done in the world" (p. 89). The Word Churches see little value in collective struggle and have moved towards European individualism as Smith (2007) contends:

> However, the individualism that is seen in the growing Word church phenomena reflects more contemporary sensibilities. The individualism that is associated with the prosperity movement reflects a capitalistic/consumerist mentality and reveals the influence of the contemporary black thematic universe. It is rooted in an underlying value placed on consumption that is reflected in its message and its resultant co-option of the Gospel in order to serve that end. (p. 147)

A growing number of Black Word Churches appear to have abrogated their ancestral responsibility as the institution that African Americans could turn to for collective leadership to help solve the larger problems facing people of African descent in America. Education, housing, health care, unemployment, and legal injustice are the areas where the Black church historically has placed its emphasis and resources toward reform. The current Word Church movement seeks to advance material interests that have little to do with social reform. Akbar (1984) argues, "The materialism which has overrun the Western mind, certainly has had its effect on the African-American mind" (p.14). Structural reform is necessary to uplift and advance the interests of people of African descent in America. This can be done by direct faith-based challenges to the existing social institutions and their exclusionary operational personalities in America. Word Churches' do not represent the original mission of Black religion as Watts (1974) argues:

> Black religion is a unique force in American life. It cannot in any way be confused or equated with American white Protestantism, Catholicism, or Judaism. It is a separate religious force in American life, different in all aspects from the tenets of the American Religious Establishment, primarily because its basis and base of operation relates exclusively to an oppressed community. (p. 25)

The abandonment of social reform issues by Word Churches in favor of material realities allows inequality to go unaddressed by the most powerful institution in the Black community. This further erodes African American agency and human potential. The material thirst that Word Churches advance and their attending emphasis on God as "divine quencher" has psychological implications for African Americans. The Word Churchs' emphasis on "individualism" is antithetical to the interests of African Americans. Smith (2007) writes:

> The growing popularity of the prosperity message in the black church in certain ways reflects materialist values and meanings. By speaking to the desire for financial gain, many of these churches teach that the Gospel message is a way to obtain personal wealth. It is clear that some forms of individualism present in the black church today are a departure from the communal sense that arose out of the conditions of the historical black thematic universe. (p. 160)

The abandonment of the communal nature of African spirituality by Word Churches places African Americans in a vulnerable position because it alienates them from the authentic sources of their spiritual strength.

Clearly, the Black church has never intentionally positioned itself as an institution to weaken the Black community, but as the material prosperity message in Word Churches grows, this possibility exists. The contemporary Black church has shifted its theological and ideological focus. After recording the views of leaders of 1,863 congregations in the Black church tradition, Rasor and Dash (2003) reported that sermon topics, music and related activities have changed from traditional emphasis to more individual prophecies:

> When the ministers were asked about the topics of their sermons, the overwhelming majority felt that their sermons "always" focus on God's love and care (83 percent), personal spiritual growth (74 percent) and practical advice on daily living (66 percent)....
> Comparatively few indicated that their sermons almost always focus on social justice (25 percent), the social situation (17 percent) or Black liberation theology or womanist theology (12 percent). (p. 49)

From an African agency standpoint what is most problematic about Word Churches is their lack of focus on social issues. The Word Churches main emphasis (material prosperity) is outside of the original concerns and historic trajectory of the Black religious and prophetic tradition. There are three fundamental characteristics of the radical tradition in Black religion according to Wilmore (1983): "1) the quest for independence from white control; 2) the revalorization of the image of Africa; and 3) the acceptance of protest and agitation as theological prerequisites for black liberation and the liberation of all oppressed peoples" (p. xiii). Exception is taken here with the word "radical" used by Wilmore. The advancement of African people is usually considered radical when it does not align itself with the interests of European and European American control structures. The original mission of Black religion in America had at its base a vigorous challenge to the unequal relationships between Black and white people (Cone, 1970; W.R. Jones, 1973; Lincoln, 1974).

Washington (1978) echoes this reality when he asserts, "Commitment to freedom, justice and equality of opportunity for all is by definition what black religion is, means and contends" (p. iv).

The position taken by Word Churches, that religious faithfulness will be rewarded by material wealth, does not exist in the original mission of Black religion. Clearly, the advancement of an ideology that centers on material wealth will not have any appreciable influence on public policy issues concerning African Americans. The most successful public policy initiatives that emanated from Black social protest have not historically had at their base the singular element of a material consciousness. This point underscores the lack of utility found in Word Churches' insistence on material attainment for African Americans. The material agenda of Word Churches compromises the African American community's ability to focus on the issues that many of them face. Concerns, such as but not limited to, racism, poverty, public school reform, job training, and affordable housing remain impediments to most Black people fulfilling their realization of agency. Ideas that do not address these disparities are not in the best interests of African Americans, collective well-being. The disproportionate amount of emphasis on material culture by Word Churches has possible psychological implications for African Americans. Azibo (2001) contends:

> Materialistic depression refers to the condition in which material goods or the lack of them serve as one's criteria for judging oneself and/or others. Victims of materialistic depression seek the accumulation of money and status symbols which they regard as having some intrinsic value above and beyond their economic value. In some cases money and items of conspicuous consumption are practically revered. (p. 87)

Azibo's analysis brings attention to the possibility that Word Churches may produce maladaptive disorders in the minds of those African Americans who uncritically adhere to the explicit materialism located in the Word Churches central message. The uncritical acceptance of the material message distracts African

Americans from the core issues facing most of them as a community. Material values by themselves will not pull African Americans together in a collective spirit of resistance. This value system creates situations where people distance themselves from those with less and at the same time produces an artificially manufactured allegiance with those who have the same as Smith (2007) maintains:

> The growth of Word churches that espouse this "name it and claim it" gospel creates attitudes that are focused on the creation and accumulation of personal wealth based upon one's faith in God and in turn, God's favor toward the individual. As a consequence positive attitudes continue toward those who have and against those who have not, this time based upon the spurious interpretation and application of Scripture. (p. 148)

The communal nature inherent in the African American cosmological spirit is neutralized by this alien set of values that determines the human worth of an individual based upon their material status. A materialistic religious orientation is counter to the strengths of the struggle that allowed people of African descent to survive and challenge the periods of enslavement, Jim Crow, legal segregation, and current European and American hegemony. The uncritical acceptance of the positions taken in Word Churches by African Americans may prove detrimental to the Black community and create a division that violates the original thrust of the Black Church. Smith (2007) asserts, "Unfortunately, this is often communicated and reinforced through worship services that pay more attention to the needs, perceived and real, of middle-class congregants than those of the poor and marginalized in the community" (p.148). Without the connection to ancient African spirituality, African American followers of the Word ministries will fall prey to spiritual positions that use God to satisfy the cravings of a material culture that are produced by the pressures of advertising and market forces inherent in the contemporary capitalist project.

Based upon their central message of materiality, Word Churches seem to find little value in the ethical prophecies of

Henry Highland Garnet, Henry M. Turner, David Walker, Nat Turner, and Dr. Martin Luther King Jr. History has recorded the fact that these men believed that divine inspiration was the driving force behind their push for self-determination of African people in their respective time periods. The major challenge facing Word Churches rests upon their inability to translate their material message into African-centered agency for the masses of marginalized Black people in America. It is possible that Word Churches have produced a situation similar to the generation of individuals who abandoned Dr. King's message of agency and self-determination, as Marable (2000b) posits:

> Part of their current dilemma is created by their conscious, class oriented commitment to infuse the Negro middle class into the present economic order and to perpetuate the inert politics of bourgeois reform. They are not prepared to repudiate the system which rewards their own political accommodation at the expense of the continued exploitation of Black working class and poor people. (p. 211)

The understanding that a singular focus on material attainments is not in the best interests of African people is an ancient observation. Ancient African sacred texts found in African antiquity penned by high sages, such as Ptah-Hotep, examined the futility found in materialism. Karenga (1984)

> If you wish your conduct to be perfect, to be free from all that is evil, guard against the vice of greed for material things. It is a grievous sickness and there is no cure for it. There can be no confidence among those infected with it. It turns a kind friend into a bitter enemy. It causes conflict with fathers, mothers and the brothers of mothers and it separates the wife from her husband. It is a bundle of all kinds of evil and a bag containing vices of every kind. Established are those whose standard is righteousness, who walk according to its ways. They shall surely prosper thereby, but the greedy will not have even a grave. (p. 44)

The ancient African sages understood the potential dangers of a disproportionate amount of emphasis on the material world. The materialist ideology does not support the African American survival thrust because it accentuates the role of individual satisfaction versus collective group advancement. If accepted uncritically this idea has the potential to move African Americans further away from the emancipatory foundation located in authentic Black religion. The idea of asking God for help in attaining the basic necessities of life is not being challenged in this work. The disproportionate emphasis on the material at the expense of the African American collective is what is being critiqued.

An ethical, democratic materiality rooted in African spirituality with an emphasis on communalism is what is absent in large measure in the Word Church movement. A return to and re-ignition of communitarian solidarity based on common faith must be part of the Word Churches' message if it is to sustain itself and be of any positive service to African Americans. A new type of pastoral care has to develop in the material doctrine presented by the Word Church. This African-centered teaching and nurturing should contain the resistive agency-driven elements drawn from the Black religious tradition that gave African Americans focus and direction during times of collective crisis. The Word Churches current ideological configuration does not meet the needs of its core constituency as Cone (1984) asserts:

> The black church, though spatially located in the community of the oppressed, has not responded to the needs of its people. It has, rather drained the community, seeking to be more like the white church. Its ministers have condemned the hopeless and have mimicked the values of whites. (p. 84)

In mimicking the values of whites the Word Church locates Black salvation in the material world. Consequently, the emphasis on the material message found in the Word Church is a contemporary ideological threat to the internal security of African Americans. It distracts and distorts their theological and ancestral responsibility to fight oppression and inequality as well as provide communal help and inspiration to the poor and unfortunate. The focus on material gains by the Word Churches absolves more fortunate Blacks of their responsibility to help others. This may lead to divisions within the Black church and has the potential to separate Black people based along social and economic lines. The original message in Black religion did not center upon the deliverance of material goods. As Akoto (1992) contends:

> If we recognize the primacy of spirituality in the cultural construct of our ancestors, then we would replace the aimlessness and emptiness of our lives with a spiritual construct appropriate to the times but consistent with the essence of ancestral traditions. (p. 76)

Absent from the central teachings of the Word Church is the insistence on sacrifice. It is unclear how the advancement of materialism addresses these fundamental concerns of African Americans, as Karenga (1999) asserts, "In a contemporary context of commercially cultivated self-indulgence and therapeutic consumerism, a morality of sacrifice becomes a central pillar in the ongoing thrust to envision and pursue possibilities of human freedom and flourishing in society, history and our lives" (pp. vii-viii). African moral philosophy is oftentimes missing from the Word Churches' teachings. Examining God's liberating activity that restores man to wholeness must be prioritized in the Word Church.

The accentuation on the material world by Word Churches erodes the historical connectedness that Black people need to be able to engage the problems that they face in America and the world. Pinn (2002) argues, "Indeed, the gospel of prosperity that is preached in the more sizeable churches may serve to hamper this national thrust" (p.138). Echoing Pinn's observation H. Harris (1997) maintains:

> There is a tendency right now among Black Church men to be at ease in Zion, to kind of feel that every thing is okay in the arena of race and social justice,

and to concentrate primarily on building our build-
ings and preaching success to our people. (p. 52)

The spirit of agitation against social injustice that was the
centerpiece of the Black church during the civil rights era does
not drive the message of the Word Church. Pinn (2002) observes,
"It is more than likely that this gospel of prosperity in a world of
economic injustice easily devolves and becomes a religious cover
for materiality, reading spiritual growth and material acquisition
as synonymous" (p.139).

The history of Black religion in America contains a legacy
of spiritual activities that have engaged, challenged, and resisted
the wrongs in society that have been perpetuated against African
Americans. The Black church has been the institution that houses
the ideas and generated the movements that sought to improve
the life chances and opportunities for people of African descent
in North America.

The contemporary development of Word Churches and
their resulting emphasis on material well being is at odds with
the history of resistance rooted in the Black religious experience
in America. The Word Church phenomenon and its message of
materiality, if accepted uncritically by African Americans, may
distract them from their ancestral responsibility to challenge the
status quo ante. Therefore, the Word Church and its material
message is located in this work as an Agency Reduction Formation.

Chapter 6

THE EUROPEAN
WORLDVIEW AND AFRICAN
DISPLACEMENT

Africans in America derive many of their contemporary realities from the displacement process of enslavement. The idea of African displacement and its lingering effects on African American reality must be considered as Clarke (1991) maintains:

> When you take people out of the cultural surround-
> ings in which they originally developed you take away
> part of their humanity. African people living outside of
> Africa are so obsessed with surviving under conditions
> that they did not create that they often lack a universal
> view of their condition and how it started" (p. 406)

Dr. Clarke speaks to the reality of African displacement and its lingering influences on African Americans. Removed by force from their native homeland early in the 17th century, the period of enslavement and its man-made artificial requirements altered the shape of African life in British North America. Stripped of their rights to live as free people, Africans in America had to adapt and adopt ways of being that were not consistent with their indigenous life practices. Africans in America were coercively introduced to alternative life designs by the exigencies of the American exploitative agrarian system, its customs, and by white supremacy.

The enslavement process attempted to dehumanize the African spirit and replace it with alien cultures, traditions, and ways of being. These ideas were completely foreign to the African principles of existence that captive Africans had known and practiced for centuries. The enslavement social structures forcefully discarded traditional African conceptions of life and submerged captive Africans in European versions of reality. The day-to-day modes of existence once solely employed by Europeans now became the legally sanctioned and authorized way of life for Africans now forced to live in North America. Enslavement saw little value in allowing Africans in America most forms of cultural retention. European American resistance to indigenous African folkways and value structures gave rise to the notion that the African had no history and no past. Herskovits (1941) maintains, "In the course of capture, importation, and enslavement they lost every vestige of the African culture" (p. 5). Although Herskovits overstates this point it remains a useful critique.

The forced abandonment of African value structures by Africans in North America has over time altered the state of nature of African Americans in the 20th and 21st centuries. Consequently, in the last three decades of the 20th century there was a reduction in the collective thrust toward communitarian agency by people of African descent in America. Looking backward Herskovits observed that, "A new life had to be formed and was formed in the pattern of the New World" (p. 5). This new life meant the abandonment of the cultural systems that had sustained African people in Africa. The New World required their African captives to be compliant with exotic human activities that did not resemble authentic versions of African life. Herskovits contended:

> ...Negroes were forced into the organization required by the plantation and by demands of the particular families to which they were attached. The only folkways that had elements in common for all the slaves were those they found among them in America. The Africans began to take hold of life where they could.

> They began to speak English, to take up the Christian religion, to fall into the labor pattern demanded by American needs and customs, to fit themselves as best they could into all the mores of the New World. (p. 5)

Clearly, it becomes necessary to understand the American Negro as a hybrid form of someone else's design. The construction of the Negro must first take place in the destruction of his native habits and cultural practices. This was done by punishing him for attempting to retain residual forms of his natural African state of nature and rewarding him for acquiescence and acceptance of alien cultural practices. A process of "seasoning" was instituted to develop the Negro in the way that was most beneficial to slaveholders. Franklin and Moss (2000) observe:

> Since slaves were constantly being brought in from Africa, overseers found it necessary to develop a practice of "breaking" in the "newcomers". In some areas the newcomers were distributed among the seasoned, or veteran, slaves whose duty it was to teach the newly arrived slaves the ways of life in the New World. In other places the newcomers were kept apart and supervised by a special staff of guardians and inspectors who were experienced in breaking in those who might offer resistance to adjusting to their new environment." (pp. 52-53)

The goal of the seasoning process was to make the captive African into a being who would not question the extraction of his African consciousness while simultaneously producing a tractable servant of plantation interests. This process is metaphorically similar to the Frankenstein folklore of American cinema and *The Modern Prometheus* in European literature. However, it departs from these two fantasies because the seasoning process has real-life applications and implications for African Americans.

Through a prescriptive process of socialization and environmental conditioning, Africans held in bondage in North America were inculcated to obey and not question foreign human concepts or alien cultural practices and to dislodge themselves from their historical memory of Africa. This was an integral part of the seasoning process. Buchanan (2002) understands this reality and speaks to it in an American context:

> Destroy the record of a people's, past, leave it in ignorance of who its ancestors were and what they did, and one can fill the empty vessels of their souls with a new history, as in 1984. Dishonor or disgrace a nation's heroes, and you can demoralize its people." (p. 147)

The seasoning process was mandated by force of arms and institutionalized by ritualized brutality against captive Africans. Bennett (1961) looks at the similarities in seasoning between Hispanic and protestant America:

> In both areas slaves were given a new conception of themselves—according to the different lights of their captors. This process, whether it took place in Brazil or harsh South Carolina, was a painful, mind reversing operation in which two or three out of ten died. In one form or another, every slave from Africa went through this "breaking-in" period. During this period, which varied from one to three years, the slave was taught pidgin English or French or Spanish. He got a new name and began to look at himself and others in a different manner. Yahweh took the place of Olorum; Legba became St. Peter; the Mass or hymnal replaced African rituals. (p. 52)

The African in America was alienated from his ancestral cultural truths in a deliberate and calculated fashion by American slaveholders to insure that plantation interests were attended to by his captive unsalaried labor force. The rules developed by the slaveholders became the customs and traditions that would shape the relationships between Blacks and whites in America. Frazier (1939) offered observations on the permanence and uniqueness of the situation facing the Africans held in bondage in America. He maintains:

> Probably never before in history has a people been so nearly completely stripped of its social heritage as the

Negroes who were brought to America. Other con-
quered races have continued to worship their household gods within the intimate circle of their kinsmen.
But American slavery destroyed household gods
and dissolved the bonds of sympathy and affection
between men of the same blood and household. Old
men and women might have brooded over memories
of their African homeland but they could not change
the world around them. Through force of circumstance, they had to acquire a new language, adopt new
habits of labor and take over, however imperfectly, the
folkways of the American environment. (p. 21)

Because of generations of compulsory behavior modifications brought to bear by mandated adherence to American
cultural requirements, the African in America has become an
American, an African American. The implied hyphen symbol-
izes a person of two worlds. The African American possesses the
genetic classification of Africa and the citizenship and cultural
realities of America. This duality has caused, according to DuBois
(1994) in the 20th century, a "double consciousness":

After the Egyptian and Indian, the Greek and
Roman, the Teuton and Mongolian, the Negro is a
sort of seventh son, born with a veil, and gifted with
the second sight in this American world—a world
which yields him no true self-consciousness, but only
lets him see himself through the revelation of the
other world. (p. 2)

The "second sight" and double consciousness that is required of
African Americans is part and parcel of their American experience. Dubois goes on to say, "It is a peculiar sensation, this double
consciousness, this sense of always looking at one's self through
the eyes of others, of measuring one's soul by the tape of a world
that looks on in amused contempt and pity" (p. 2). The necessity
for this behavior was forced upon African Americans by their
involuntary displacement from their native land of Africa and
vibrates throughout their consciousness in the 21st century.

AFRICAN AMERICANS' ALIEN STATE OF NATURE

Because of the prolonged exposure to alien value structures that removed them from their original African ways of being, many African Americans adopted the European worldview construct to guide their vision of the world. My contention is that the abandonment of the core principles of African worldview and the resulting non-African worldview orientation alienates African Americans from the sources of their original strength. This is reflected in the fragmentation, cultural mis-orientation, and general malaise that is present in many segments of the Black community (Kambon, 1992, 1998). These anti-African reaction formations that African Americans engage in may lead to an abrogation of their ancestral responsibility to continue the collective struggle for all people of African descent as Beatty (2002) argues:

> African people fundamentally understand the world in terms of we, in terms of the interrelatedness and interconnectedness of the Creator, cosmos, society, and the person. This view determines what we see as truth, how we see truth, and act upon the world with this truth." (p. 213)

Because of the lack of a collective African-centered dialectic and the continued disengagement from African worldview African Americans are without a proper human compass to orient themselves in the world (Asante, 1998; Kambon, 1992). Through an aggressive system of human social engineering known as assimilation, Blacks in America for generations have been symbolically assimilated through the institutionalization of the European worldview operating in the American cultural ethos. Post-racialism seeks to inculcate African Americans to recognize little value in collective racial strategies of resistance against domination. This assumption is predicated on the mythical assertion that America is race neutral in form and practice.

These shifts in worldview have brought consequences for African people in America. The assimilation process requires the African in America to seek out the so-called universal principles of American culture. This position was advanced in the mid-20th century by E. Franklin Frazier (1957) but future historical realties would challenge Frazier's assertion:

> Since the institutions, the social stratification, and the culture of the Negro community are essentially the same as those of the larger community, it is not strange that the Negro minority belongs among the assimilationist rather than the pluralist, secessionist, or militant minorities. It is seldom that one finds Negroes who think of themselves as possessing a different culture from whites and that their culture should be preserved. (p.681)

Strong exception is here taken with Frazier's assessment considering the development of Afrocentric, Pan-African, nationalist, and separatist survival formations by African Americans that continue to challenge Frazier's observations. The uncritical acceptance of so-called universal American principles by African Americans dislodges them from the best practices of their African cultural origins. According to Paris (1995), "Africans and African Americans share a common worldview, which comprises a cosmological whole and unites all of life in and among the realms of spirit, history, and nature" (p. 129). Marginalization of traditional African practices brought to bear by the pressures of American culture and its resultant effects on African Americans are illuminated by Asante (1998): "If we have lost anything, it is our cultural centeredness; that is, we have been moved off our own platforms. This means that we cannot truly be ourselves or know our potential since we exist in a borrowed space" (p. 8).

The parochial vision of assimilation for African Americans by American culture placed Blacks in a dichotomous position. On the one hand they are genetically African but on the other hand they are being inculcated by American cultural restraints to be solely American. This confusion resulted in DuBois' (1994) identification of double consciousness: "One ever feels his two-ness, -- an American, a Negro; two souls, two thoughts, two unreconciled strivings; two warring ideals in one dark body, whose dogged strength alone keeps it from being torn asunder" (p. 2). The demands placed on the African American to submerge him self in all things American brought with it a plethora of challenges. The African American must now re-create his self-concept based on principles located outside of his natural state of nature.

The European worldview is not consistent with the African worldview. Worldview is defined by Wimberly and Wimberly (1986) as

> The worldview is an implicit or explicit system of values, beliefs, attitudes and expectations that influence the behavior of persons. It helps the person find his or her place in life, orders life in meaningful ways, and provides communication among people. (p. 94)

Kambon (1998) operationalizes worldview as "the mega-conceptual ideological framework derived from a racial group's cosmology which projects their reality, history, culture, philosophy (ontology, axiology, epistemology-science, etc.)/survival thrust as the center of the universe" (p. 533). Scholars (Baldwin, 1980, 1985; Baldwin & Hopkins, 1990; Myers, 1993, 1999) have examined worldview.

The European worldview was effectively transferred to white Americans in the Americas through its embedding in the cultural and institutional apparatus. European worldview is distinctly reflected in white American customs, traditions, values, mores, and accepted ways of conducting most facets of their human activities within American culture. The maintenance and transfer of African worldview to the captive African in America was disrupted by the enslavement period and its resulting seasoning processes. African worldview retention was first denied in America by the plantation systems social and economic structure. As has been discussed, African worldview maintenance was further disrupted by the assimilation process of the 20th century. In the 21st century it is being attacked again by the post-racial Agency Reduction Formations that have been identified in previous chapters of this work.

Clearly, there is a profound difference between the European American worldview and African worldview. Because of these differences it becomes necessary to explore the influence that

European worldview has had on African Americans. To date there does not exist a significant body of literature that suggests a point in world history where African Americans through force of arms or institutionalized social structures have successfully coerced Europeans or their American descendants to adopt or adapt to the African worldview. Akbar (1984) addresses this issue: "In highlighting the slavery influences we are demonstrating a distinct determinant of African-American psychological functioning which makes us unique in some of the causative influences on our actions" (p. 4). Therefore, this analysis will center on the influence of European Worldview on African Americans.

The differing world histories of European Americans and African Americans produced distinct differences in how they collectively view reality. Asante (1998) brings attention to the possibility that many white Americans have been seduced by "The structural elements of a hierarchical society that fails to recognize African agency" (p. 8). A critical understanding of this is vital to understand because European Americans have enslaved African Americans. The reverse has not occurred in American history. Senegalese scholar Cheikh Anta Diop's research articulated the view that social systems derive and evolve out of specific climatic and environmental conditions. His work suggests that these realities predispose the inhabitants to a particular worldview (Diop, 1974, 1989). This static fact altered the way Blacks and whites operate in America. This phenomenom was made clear by Diop (1974):

> The history of humanity will remain confused as long as we fail to distinguish between the two early cradles in which Nature fashioned the instincts, temperament, habits, and ethical concepts of the two subdivisions before they met each other after a long separation dating back to prehistoric times. (p. 111)

After examining thousands of years of historical, climatic and environmental patterns, Diop illuminates the point that long before the enslavement period of the New World, nature had bestowed upon Africans and Europeans distinctly different ways of being. Building on the scholarship of Diop, Kambon

(1998) developed the Comparative Worldviews Schematic. Kambon articulates three distinct worldview differences for European/European-American worldview and African/African (American) worldview. For a more extensive analysis of the worldview schematic see Kambon (1998, p. 130). The schematic is divided into three distinct parts: ethos, values and customs, and psycho-behavioral modality. In the area of ethos, Kambon (1998) argues that European/European American worldview centers upon "control/mastery over nature" and "survival of the fittest", whereas, African/African (American) worldview rests upon "oneness/harmony with nature" and "survival of the group" (p. 130). In terms of values and customs, the European/ European-American worldview is defined by "competition-individual rights", while, African/African (American) worldview is grounded in "cooperation-collective responsibility" (p. 130). In the last area of worldview, psycho-behavioral modality, Euro-pean/European-American worldview is operationalized as "individualism" and "uniqueness-differences", as opposed to African/ African (American) "groupness" and "sameness-commonality" (p. 130). My goal here is not to advance the idea that one way of being is better or worse, but to highlight the influence and ramifications of these differences on African Americans. The de-centering of the enslaved Africans continued in the Americas far beyond the actual physical bondage period. The binding social tenets of African life so vital to the existence of Africans in Africa were neutralized in North America by the prescriptive behavioral doctrines of American white supremacy and its restrictive social structures (Foner & Mahoney, 1995). Consequently, acquiescence to new maps of meaning was the white-approved survival route open to people of African descent in the American context. The prevalence of ideological hegemony and legal sanction in American culture gave most African Americans little choice except to adapt to the exigencies of the non-African world.

African American Worldview Adaptation

The influence of European worldview was not an idea that developed later as time went on, but began in the first stage of African bondage in the Americas as Coombs (1972) observes:

> The American experiment had begun and consisted mainly of white men with a European heritage. The African was of a different color, had a different language, a different religion, and had an entirely different worldview. But perhaps the most striking contrast was that, while the European came voluntarily in search of greater individual opportunity, the African came in chains. Because the European was the master and thereby the superior in the relationship, he assumed that his heritage was also superior. (p. 15)

African worldview orientation for the African American is vitality important for survival. Myers (1993) writes:

> Why is the nature of the way we view the world so important? It is important because it ultimately determines our experience, our history. All people view the world based upon a particular belief system which at another level, is structured by a conceptual system, i.e., the philosophical assumptions and principles on which one's beliefs are based. Often, these assumptions are not part of our conscious awareness; yet, the assumptions shape our beliefs. The conceptual system through which we relate to reality determines the way we perceive, think, feel, and experience the world. (p. 5)

In his comparative worldview schematic Kambon (1998) locates "groupness" as the normal/natural pattern of African American psycho-behavioral modality in the African worldview system. This is oppositional to the European behavioral modality of individualism. Because of the imposition of the European worldview which is normalized and reflected in the societal scripts and operational ethos of American culture, many African Americans adhere to a European worldview construct and adopt individualism as their self-concept. The static requirements of American culture engender acquiescence to an alien worldview by many African Americans. Submission to a non-African worldview is a necessary component of survival in America for African-Americans in most cases. An individualistic self-concept is not consistent with African Worldview as Azibo (2001) contends:

> Africans who practice and/or profess the European-centered "rugged individual" ethic are suffering from individualism. Individualism also entails the desire and practice of being unique or different and "looking out for number one" primarily. It is acutely at variance with the African-centered ethic of survival of the tribe, collective responsibility and the extended self-concept. (p. 88)

The exigencies of American white supremacy, Jim Crow, and legal segregation have historically reminded African Americans of the utility of African principles of life found in antiquity. We depended on the basic tenets of African worldview to see us through oppressive historical time periods where European worldview would not have been possible, or served our interests. The communal nature of the African worldview gives African Americans the necessary cohesion required to share resources, build alliances, and forge ahead toward their right to exist as equal members of the human family.

European worldview does not speak to the needs of African Americans because it does not emanate from their collective social or cultural history in the world. It appears to have a negative influence on African Americans as Quigley (1966) argues, "The destructive impact of Western Civilization upon so many other societies rests on its ability to demoralize their ideological and spiritual culture as much as its ability to destroy them in a material sense with firearms" (p.14). The disproportionate amount of emphasis on European worldview found in American cultural practices and social mores may have a deleterious influence on African Americans. E.P. Skinner (1999) maintains:

> The self-doubt that arose among African peoples led
> them to lose that simple human pride that normally
> prevented people from readily accepting the notion
> that they and their culture were inferior to others.
> Generations of African peoples experienced the onus
> of seeing themselves through the eyes of others. (p. 29)

The imposition of European worldview on African Americans and its corollary effects leaves some African Americans in a state of functional confusion. Predicated by the utilization and absorption of non-African worldviews some African Americans may develop "social amnesia" according to A.N. Wilson (1993):

> When we suffer from social amnesia we identify with
> abstractions: I am not Black; I am not Afrikan; I am
> a human being. I am an American. Sterile, abstract
> identity. The closer we get to it the less we see of it,
> and the more we recognize that it has no meaning.
> "What is that? Who is that? What does that stand
> for? What does it mean? It's empty, and people who
> identify themselves with these abstractions are also
> empty and experience their lives as empty, as people
> who have no feelings. They identify with the abstrac-
> tion so as to escape feelings. Therefore, we see them
> detached and cut-off from themselves as persons, as
> well as from their people. (p. 40)

The identification with abstractions that Wilson contends leads to a mind-set that places some African Americans in positions to disproportionately serve the interests of others outside of their own ethnic group.

The European worldview contains social mechanisms that are not suited to the unique collective history of people of African descent in America. The legacy of the enslavement period produced situations that required captive Africans in America to call upon the salient features of the African worldview. In order to survive in the midst of strident white supremacy, communalism or "groupness" is best suited to address the needs of Africans in times of crisis (Kambon, 1998). The individualistic self-concept inherent in European worldview was/is not in the best interests of

African Americans who historically had/have to share resources to meet the demands of an unequal society.

The cultural requirements of American citizenship have usually not rewarded African Americans for positively embracing African worldview as Kennedy (1959) argues: "According to legend, the United States of America is a "melting-pot" of the peoples of the world. The fact is, however, that the ingredients which have gone into the pot have been carefully screened for whiteness" (p. 37). Fitting in for Blacks has always been of high concern as Franklin and Moss (2000) argue: "The problem of what to do with blacks who would not adjust to American life was an old one" (p. 187). Captive Africans in America fought against the inhumane treatment they received in early American life. They later resisted all of the forms of white supremacy entrenched in its institutions, structures, and systems, but in addition they were fighting against the infliction of the European worldview on their psychological infrastructures and total existence. The acknowledgment of the influence of an alien worldview and its impact on African Americans has not gone unnoticed by African- centered scholars as Ani (1994) maintains:

> The secret Europeans discovered early in their history
> is that culture carries rules for thinking, and that if
> you could impose your culture on your victims you
> could limit the creativity of their vision, destroying
> their ability to act with will and intent in their own
> interest. (p. 1)

The relationship between culture, power, and its bearing on worldview constructs has been examined by scholars (Barrett, 2002; Cummins, 2005; Huntington, 2003; A.N. Wilson, 1998). The power that is inherent in European worldview that is perpetuated and maintained by the operational ethos of American culture, has the capacity to shape and alter the way African Americans see and act in society. Using a Weberian perspective Barrett (2002) describes power this way: "...power is the capacity of an individual to impose his or her will on another despite resistance" (p. 20). Barrett illuminates one of the central tenets of

Afrocentric theory as Asante (1998) maintains: "Our existential relationship to the culture that we have borrowed defines what and who we are at any given moment" (p. 8). Because a large number of African people were forcefully dislocated from their native homeland, a new system of understanding the world had to be learned for their survival. I am not arguing against that point. However, I am advancing the idea that the disproportionate amount of emphasis and the cultural mandates of the European worldview along with its corollary individualistic self-concept has altered the communal nature of some African Americans. Consequently, as Cummins (2005) contends,

> If through your projections, you can erode the extended family and promote a culture of individualistic material, you will have eroded the populace's last real source of security and will foster an ideology that creates a predatory cannibalistic social environment that eats itself alive, without conscious awareness that its demise is orchestrated by you. (p. 299)

Due to the legacy of white supremacy and oppression in America against them, African Americans as a group have had to possess a highly developed survival thrust. The capability for collective survival strategies is not unique to African Americans as an ethnic group, although its duration and necessity stand alone as one of their defining principles as a race of people. African American survival mechanisms most pointedly display themselves in the worldview paradigm of their ancestral heritage located in their cosmology. African cosmology is vital to the African experience. Kambon (1998) describes African cosmology as, "...the structure of reality from a particular racial-cultural perspective of experience" (p.121).

The particularity of the African American experience in America lends itself to a version of reality that is based in their collective historical experiences from Africa as well as their struggle against oppression in America as Kambon (1998) asserts:

> In abnormal-unnatural circumstances, i.e., those which we identify with a group that is not our indig-

145

enous cultural group (such as an alien group, or an acquired alien group identity), then the conception of reality out of which we operate is not naturally our own. (p. 119)

The abnormality of an imposed alien worldview distorts reality for African Americans because it artificially ordains and exists outside of their human histories. Because of their widely different experiences in the world that have been shaped by being on the opposite sides of a power dynamic, the most beneficial natural state of nature for African Americans is actualized through African cosmology and African worldview.

The state of nature position that I argue here bears no relationship in any form to the contested states of nature argument inherent in the philosophy and writings of European thinkers such as: John Locke, Thomas Hobbes, or Jean-Jacques Rousseau. No time will be spent on these ideas because they exist for different purposes than I am advancing here. My argument in this work is advocated by other scholars who have addressed the significance of African worldviews specificity and particularity for African Americans (Akbar, 1984; Ani, 1994; Baldwin & Hopkins, 1990; Diop, 1974; Nobles, 1980). The broken continuity resulting from the displacement of Africans from Africa to America and the resulting forced dislocation from indigenous African cultural systems has profound implications for African Americans.

THE IMPOSITION OF EUROPEAN WORLDVIEW

The structural and cultural imposition of the European worldview has altered the state of nature of many African Americans. For the purposes of this work I am operationalizing "state of nature" as "the historically rooted behavioral practices located in African principles of life, exemplified in African cosmology and the African worldview construct." Many of the anti-African behaviors that can be observed in this community are possible because many African Americans are living outside of the African worldview construct.

The greater the distance African Americans are from our natural state of nature, the further we are away from the sources of our strength. The culturally specific imposition of a non-African worldview in America has influenced the Sakhu of many African Americans. Nobles (2006) "Sakhu is an ancient term from Ancient Kemet, which means understanding, illumination, the eye/the soul of being" (p. 245). The individualistic self-concept inherent in the European worldview when exclusively employed by African Americans disrupts their ancestral sense of communalism and modifies the ways they engage each other in the world. Sakhu disruption alters the soul of African Americans and reduces their sense of responsibility for each other's collective well-being. The advantages of pooling resources so common during enslavement, the post-Civil War period, Jim Crow, segregation, and the pre-civil rights period are nullified by the absorption and wholesale utilization of the European worldview, because of its emphasis on individualism. Ani (1994) contends, "Culture carries rules for thinking" (p. 1). The imposition of the European worldview by American culture reshapes the consciousness of African Americans and leads to an individualistic cultural misorientation that is detrimental to the collective advancement of African Americans.

The potential incarceration of the African American mind through the European worldview dates back to the period of enslavement as observed by Akbar (2008) who states, "The process of human slavery is ultimately a psychological process by which the mind of a people is gradually brought under the control of their captors and they become imprisoned by the loss of the consciousness (awareness) of themselves" http://www.naimakbar.com/index.cfm?pageId=3. The loss of consciousness revealed in Akbar's analysis exposes one of the central dangers of the European worldview for African Americans. The European worldview did not emerge from the history or culture of African American people. It is out of synch with their ancestral realities; therefore, it does not extend to them the most beneficial means for existence in an unequal American society. This point is illuminated by Sutherland (1997):

> These values were instilled into our personality structures and incorporated into the African communi-

ties primarily as a function of the enslavement trade, colonial rule, and perpetual White domination. There is obviously a need for Africans to be resocialized to their authentic cultural traditions. (p. 125)

The posing of European worldview as universal contains elements of domination at its core. J.M. Jones (1972) observes, "More significantly, any person, regardless of his cultural background, who cannot function well according to the dictates of white Western cultural norms does not have much opportunity for success in this society" (p. 7). White Western norms are located inside of European worldview. By virtue of its unrelenting imposition it requires that people of African descent who seek its validation in order to be successful on American terms must abandon to a large extent their African historical and ancestral cultural truths. African worldview represents the natural African American ethos, because it exemplifies the authentic culturally inspired African ways of being as Asante (1998) contends, "Moreover, Africa is at the heart of all African American behavior" (p. 59). Taking exception with Asante I maintain that Africa "should" be at the heart of all African American behavior, but because of the imposition of European worldview in many cases it is not. The European worldview is adventitious to the well-being of African Americans because it takes them out of their natural rhythms of life. The cultural hegemony existing inside of the European worldview displays itself through the idea that one race of peoples' (white) culture is superior to others in the American context. Semmes (1992) contends:

> I define cultural hegemony as the systemic negation of one culture by another. By this process I mean that the internal dynamics of one culture evolves in such a way that it calls into dissolution the independence, coherence, and viability of another culture to which it has a socio-historical connection. In a sense, the one culture bases its existence and well-being on the ability to absorb, redirect, or redefine institution building and symbol formation in the other. (p. 1).

Worldview produces the conditions that influence thought and in the same vein these influences determine behavior. The congealing of the non-African worldview in the minds of many African Americans may lead to a wide-scale atomization of their ancestral responsibility to engage in collective struggle against the injustice and inequality that persists in America.

SOCIAL REALITY

In any society there exists a reality that has been created by the development of a cultural axis. Those involved in the human activity of a community revolve around the dominant cultural axis and follow it for continuity of the given cultures requirements and objectives. So-called normalized American cultural functioning is predicated on the universality of European worldview and its resultant behavioral standards. The provincialism that is inherent in European worldview has borne a fundamental relationship between the European worldview and social dominance theory (SDT). According to Sidanius and Pratto (1999), "SDT begins with the basic observation that all human societies tend to be structured as systems of group-based social hierarchies" (p. 31). Because of the legacy of the period of African enslavement in America and its structural aftermaths, African Americans were not figured democratically into the group-based hierarchies of America. Consequently, American assimilation as a project has not lived up to its promise as far as African Americans are concerned. Assimilation requires abandonment of a group's native cultural core elements as Schaefer (2005) argues, "Assimilation is very difficult. The person must forsake his or her cultural tradition to become part of a different, often antagonistic culture" (p. 29). Schaefer continues, "In public discussions today, assimilation is the ideology of the dominant group in forcing people how to act" (p. 30).

The forcing of behavior that Schaefer argues is made possible by the imposition of European worldview in the public and cultural spheres of the United States. As an element of European worldview, individualism has historically shown little promise for the well-being of African Americans as Coombs (1972) asserts: "The racist attitudes of mainstream America, both North and South, made it almost impossible for a Negro to conceive of himself purely in individualistic terms" (p. 155). The racialized structural reality of American inequality and the robust imposition of European worldview make it clear that African Americans in order to thrive en masse must revisit and continue their African-based ancestral traditions centered in a communal existence in order to effectively serve their collective interests. African worldview has been disrupted by the enslavement period, neutralized by symbolic assimilation, and rhetorically addressed but not actualized by the 21st century ideology of the Post-Racial Project. All of the aforementioned social systems reduce the agency advancement and communitarian survival thrust of African Americans by reducing their potential for collective resistance against inequality.

The argument has been made that Blacks and whites share a common culture dating back to slavery so there is no need for separate ways of being as Payne (1998) contends: "For more than 375 years, blacks and whites have fashioned their common culture. The institution of slavery could not have existed without the daily interaction of slaves and slaveholders" (p. 56). Payne does not examine or give mention to the acute power dynamic that was entrenched in the period of enslavement. He also neglects the historical reality that enslavement was not a voluntary exercise for African people. The institution of slavery would not have been possible without the brute physical forces of white supremacy. Categorically, African enslavement was coerced unsalaried labor that assaulted the humanity of African people by denying them their rights to basic human freedoms. Payne's argument is attempting to advance an ahistorical utopian speculation that seeks to demonstrate a nonexistent democratic relationship between captive Africans and their European-descended American captors. The development of a so-called "common culture" that was developed by the exigencies of the period of enslavement does not suggest a voluntary natural blending of cultures. It does connote an artificially man made manufacturing of an alien cultural reality that was forced on African people without their consent. Chafe, Korstad, Ortiz, Parrish, Ritterhouse, Roberts, and Davis (2001) assert, "The politics of white supremacy, that decreed by legislation and custom that African Americans remain in a subordinate place in American society, meant that history itself was transformed into a terrain of cultural and social struggle" (p. 58). In the early and mid-20th century, the de jure institutionalization of inequality in America along with the advancement of the melting-pot idea that was advanced in American life resulted in a unique form of cultural hegemony.

The emergence of American cultural hegemonic practices influenced African American ways of life as R. Neville (2003) argues, "The American way of life is not negotiable. Worse-the American way of life is inescapable" (p. 19). The non-negotiability of American life carries with it elements of social reality control for African Americans. Baldwin (1980) contends:

> Euro-American culture has therefore attempted to force the legitimacy of the European system of social reality on black people, by superimposing their system on our African system of social reality. ...In short, Europeans control the formal process of social reinforcements. Control over this vital process is the key to the power of Euro-American control over (and/or obscuring of) black peoples social reality. It allows Euro-American culture to superimpose a consistent stream of Eurocentric definitions and their experiential confirmations on the experiences of black people in this society. (p.101)

The adoption of alien, foreign, and exotic systems of social reality places African Americans at acute variance with their optimal states of nature (Azibo, 2001; Myers, 1993). As has been stated, African worldview is the original state of nature for African Americans. This worldview has provided authentic ways of being and advanced the survival thrust of African people in both Africa and America, when it is actualized by people of African descent. African worldview is the normative behavioral and cultural ethos for African Americans and exists outside of the forced exigencies of surviving in a dominative environment. At the base of successful movements of self-determination of people of African descent are the basic tenets of African worldview. Prolonged exposure to alien worldviews of non-African, non-melanated people in some cases has led to psychological trauma for some African Americans according to Leary (2005) who asserts, "The legacy of trauma is reflected in many of our behaviors and our beliefs..." (p. 121). An uncritical, disproportionate level of acceptance of the European worldview, which is based on the self-concept of individualism, could be understood as a primary cause of the reduced collective desire for large-scale communitarian agency-directed activities in the African American community.

Therefore, I am locating the European worldview construct as an Agency Reduction Formation. The free moral agency of African Americans is compromised when they are heavily invested in individualism. The seductive influence of the non-African worldview has compromised the cultural autonomy of people of African descent in America. Tomlinson (1991) puts forth this analysis of cultural autonomy: "The principal of cultural auton-omy holds, roughly, that a culture has the right to 'self-legislation' and freedom from heteronomous control. Domination here is the exercise of such autonomy: manipulation or control of the culture from outside" (p. 95). The enslavement period placed the African in an alien environment (Bennett, 1961). This displace-ment forced indigenous Africans to live outside of their estab-lished practices and absorb foreign ways of being.

The damage from this exotic unnatural state of nature con-tinues to inform the realities and behavioral choices of African Americans. This can be seen in their adoption of the divisive self-concept of individualism, which is at the core of the separations that are observable in African American life. When individualism is uncritically embraced by large segments of the African American community, it is usually at the expense of other people of African descent. The individualistic ethos emanating from the European worldview disrupts and compromises the communal nature expressed in the African worldview as Paris (1995) maintains:

> Commensurate with their African roots, African Americans have borne no small disdain for the phi-losophy of individualism and the cultural spirit it has fostered. They have had similar contempt for the

logical extension of such a philosophy in the moral development of self-centered persons who pursue their own autonomous purposes with little or no regard for the well-being of others. Such persons, morally shaped in accordance with the principle of individual autonomy, differ sharply from those who are formed in consonance with a historical principle of communal belonging. The thought of the former sacrificing either their own lives or even a substantial part of their property for the good of others is totally repulsive to them. By contrast, the communal traditions of African Americans (deeply rooted in Africa and preserved through slavery in the family, music, and religion) have made it psychologically impossible for the vast majority of them to embrace fully the basic value system of white Americans. Consequently, the predominant moral and religious values of the two groups differ sharply, a difference clearly manifested in their respective thought about person, family, community, and religion, as well as their understandings of music, property, and politics. (p. 126)

Represented in European worldview are ideas and ways of being that do not speak to the psychological and historical realities of African Americans (Myers, 1993). The Black experience in America is housed in the twin ideas of resistance and agency. This is the basic organizing principle located in the historiography of African Americans beginning with the forced dislocation of our ancestors from Africa in the 16th century, to the systemic inequalities still present in the 21st century. Because of this, historically African American behavior has traditionally evolved in a collective and communal load-sharing fashion. This worldview has served this population well when implemented in times of crisis. Because of their racialized placement outside of the structural, systemic, and institutional realms of the political economy that emanated from the Americas, to the lingering plague of racism present in the 21st century; African Americans should be invested in the idea of communitarian self-help strategies that are actualized in African worldview. Communal ways of being represent the normal/natural historical and behavioral ethos of people of African descent in America (Paris, 1995).

I am not suggesting that one worldview is superior to others as Myers also (1993) observes: "Though we are speaking of a generalized cultural world view, we are not assuming that all people of European descent think sub-optimally or are racist/sexist; we are not discounting individual differences" (p.11). However, I am vigorously advancing the idea that because of the different collective histories between European-descended Americans and African-descended Americans, along with the current racialized challenges that African Americans face in America, it is in their best interests to adhere to the worldview construct that has historically served their interests, which is the African worldview.

Because of the direct imposition of European worldview on the lives of African Americans, many of them have absorbed and adopted a "sub-optimal conceptual system" based on materialism. (Myers, 1993) maintains:

> Starting with the basic ontological assumption that the nature of reality is principally material, we are set up for a world view in which the resources for survival exist in only a finite and limited amount (e.g., the pie is only so big). (p. 10)

Ingrained in the non-African view of social reality is an individualistic approach that is centered on the material. This idea is anti-African because it is in direct violation of the ancestral beliefs of African people. Communalism and its surrounding realities are the backbone of a healthy African American existence. Speaking to this reality Davidson (1969) asserts:

> Though couched in mythopoeic terms these approaches to reality, these 'theories of the actual', were linked to practical use. They bore on the craft community relations as hoe culture bore on the growing of food, or weaving on the production of clothes. They were ideological supports for socio-moral charters of a specific form and content, conceptual offspring of a particular time and space. Anything but arbitrary,

they were 'the religious extrapolations of the experiences generated in the relationships between parents
and children in societies with a social organization
based on kinship and descent', and one may add, of
an economic organization embedded in subsistence
and mutual aid. Within the kinship continuum, they
offered 'a finished whole which embraces all activity,
whether social, technical, or economic'. (p. 175)

The sharing of resources, talents, and information has been
an a priori fact of existence for people of African descent for
as long as white supremacy and structural inequality have had
a place in America, beginning in British North America (Paris,
1995). The uncritical acceptance of the European worldview
compromises the moral compass of African Americans because
it reduces their level of responsibility to the collective matrix of
people of African descent, both in America and Africa.

THE EUROPEAN WORLDVIEW'S INFLUENCE ON AFRICAN AMERICAN VALUES

The consequences surrounding the wholesale adoption of a
non-African worldview by African Americans have meaning and
impact in the 21st century. The millennium poses unique challenges for people of African descent. Popular culture, specifically
the genre of music labeled "rap" or hip-hop has in one of its forms
been saturated with the European worldview. It has been reported
that 97.7 percent of African American youth listen to rap music
(MEE Productions, 1993).Tricia Rose (1994) defines hip-hop as
"Hip Hop is a cultural form that attempts to negotiate the experience of marginalization, brutally truncated opportunity, and
oppression within the cultural imperatives of African American
and Caribbean history, identity and community" (p. 21). Boyd,
(2003) argues, "This is why hip hop is so important, and why it
speaks to so many. It is at once humorous and a weapon of guerilla
warfare against the sophisticated technology of the dominant
order" (p. 143). Originally, this form of music articulated and
exposed the quality-of-life disparities between people of African

descent and non-African people. Hip-hop has morphed into a mainstream cultural and consumer product with wide-ranging appeal. No longer lodged within the confines of resistance and illumination of grievances against the status quo, contemporary hip-hop contains different genres of expression within it.

The genre most clearly articulating the basic tenets of the European worldview, is corporate controlled "non-conscious rap" (McQuillar, 2007). The explicit lyrics and communicative ideas of this genre are centered upon the twin goals of individualistic and materialistic self aggrandizement. This position is diametrically opposed to the early expositors of political or conscious rap who demanded attention to the abandonment and marginalization of the African American community, located in post-industrial urban America. The lack of positive attention given to the African American community by the Ronald Reagan administration of 1980-1988 resonated throughout the early forms of conscious rap. McQuillar operationalizes "conscious rap" as "Songs that are responsible, thought provoking, and/or inspirational against social justice" (p. 2). At its core non-conscious rap contains none of these elements. Fernando (1994) maintains that music is more than entertainment he holds, "Some people consider music as pure entertainment, when in fact, it is one of the most intimate reflections of a culture" (p. xi). In the case of non-conscious rap most African forms of cultural reflection that Fernando argues for are absent in terms of it mirroring African worldview or culture.

In public discourse the subject of young Black male behavior is unavoidable. What is not so common is an African-centered analysis of the causal relationship of the challenges that are facing young Black males. By virtue of its artistic attachment to European worldview, non-conscious rap does not transmit authentic African cultural values and virtues to the segment of this population that listens to it.

Consequently, maladaptive behavioral manifestations are resulting as a consequence of the listener's immersion and internalization of the values inherent in this particular form of rap music. The alien values embedded in non-conscious rap influences the types of behaviors that African-American youth may determine have value. Located within the "Cool Pose" Majors and Bilson (1992) value system are non-African demeanors and behaviors that are counterproductive to the well-being of the African American community. Many of these values are reflective of European worldview and its widespread effects on American culture. Majors and Bilson contend, "In twentieth century life, which some observers argue is plagued by anomie, we are surrounded by a culture that places an inordinate value on materialism, success, prestige, personal possessions, and wealth. Conspicuous consumption is no longer unusual" (pp. 5-6).

Non-conscious rap translates alien European worldview cultural values and realities to young Black males. The awareness of the physical degradations inherent in genocide and homicide is well established in Black communities (Asante, 2003b). However, the mental and behavioral manifestations termed "mentacide", (B.E. Wright, 1984, p. 35), which is instigated by the dual components of oppression and, I argue, non-conscious rap are in need of illumination. Wright operationalized mentacide as "the deliberate and systematic destruction of a groups mind with the ultimate purpose being the extirpation of that group" (p. 35). Because non-conscious rap has become one of the major influences in the lives of some young Black males, it is possible to infer that they are transferring the non-African messages from this art form into their behavior, which may be leading to distorted identity formations in some cases. A.N. Wilson (1992) contends that Black males who are responding to oppression and white male authority develop resistive behaviors. I am advancing here the reality that the Eurocentric ideas embedded in non-conscious rap music have led to what Wilson has defined as "reactionary masculinity" (p. 34). According to Wilson reactionary masculinity has several characteristics of which I will highlight three in no particular order of importance:

1. Lacks a deep and abiding Afrikan identity and consciousness; exhibits an impoverished empathy for others.
2. Is a conspicuous consumer; consumer-oriented— concerned mainly with parasitically exploiting

others, works merely to earn "spending money" i.e. money to spend irresponsibly; is "into flashy clothes, cars, fads, and styles of all types.

3. Motivated and defined by self-alienation; exhibits an absence of self-knowledge; ignorance of his ethnic heritage; unbounded hedonism; narcissistic drives; deep insecurities regarding the reality of his masculinity and his masculine courage. (pp. 34-35)

Wilson's observations highlight at the behavioral level the possible maladaptive behavioral manifestations that may occur when a young Black male has absorbed and adopted uncritically just two components of the European worldview construct: individualism and materialism through non-conscious rap.

Kambon's (1998) concept of worldview in which he articulates the basic tenets and differences between European and African worldviews serves as a guide for this understanding. A possible linkage can be drawn from the shift in value constructions (i.e., African to European) by African Americans and the challenges they are now currently facing in the larger world (Asante, 1998, 2003b). The value shift in African American communities may be related to their low level of African self-consciousness. According to Kambon (1992) there are four primary indicators of African self-consciousness or ASC:

a. Awareness of one's African identity (a collective consciousness) and African cultural heritage, and sees value in the pursuit of knowledge of Self.

b. Recognition of African survival and positive development as one's number one priority.

c. Respect for and active perpetuation of things African; African life and African cultural institutions.

d. Maintaining a standard of conduct of resolute and uncompromising resistance to all things "anti-African" (p. 55).

Prolonged exposure to European worldview may lead to a reduction in ASC in African Americans (Kambon, 1992; Azibo, 2001). Low levels of ASC may cause an uncritical and disproportionate level of acceptance of the inherent meanings displayed in non-conscious rap. Jamison (2006) argues:

> In its early development formation, ASC can be derailed from its natural African survival thrust potential by bombardment from alien/anti African social-environmental experiences, such as the dominance of Eurocentric values and beliefs in one's formative experiences. When this kind of aberrant development occurs, it can, in extreme cases, result in the internalization of an alien self-consciousness overriding the underdeveloped ASC, creating a negative health condition called cultural misorientation (CM). (p. 49)

It is of critical importance for African Americans to understand the relationship between non-conscious rap, European worldview, and the combined negative influences that they both have on their lives. Jamison maintains, "The best of rap music rejects the cultural norms and standards superimposed on African Americans by mainstream Euro-American society. While, at its "worst" rap music is no more than a reflection of Euro-American values" (p. 47). Exception is here being taken with Jamison's all-inclusive use of the term "rap." In terms of research specificity I am isolating and centering on the form of rap called "non-conscious" as previously operationalized by McQuillar (2007). This isolation is critical because it identifies the specific form of rap music that is being investigated without castigating the entire art form. Other scholars have examined the usefulness of this approach Kitwana (1994) asserts that, "The researcher is able to isolate various tendencies and examine them more carefully" (p. 42). Non-conscious rap advances European worldview. B.F. Skinner (1969) argued, "The wealth of a culture depends upon the productive behavior of its members" (p.19). Consequently, it is necessary to examine the influence of non-conscious rap on African Americans. This particular art form is worthy of investigation because of the messages it conveys to its core audience. According to Roopali Mukherjee (2006):

> With diamonds, mink, and champagne, black
> popular culture has, in recent years, made an auda-
> cious spectacle of conspicuous commodity consump-
> tion. Commonly termed 'bling', the 'ghetto fabulous'
> aesthetic of these flashy displays has prompted
> vociferous debate about the cultural meanings of
> contemporary black consumerism. Is it pathological?
> Subversive? Deviant? (p. 1)

Mukherjee illuminates the possibility that the values in
African American life and culture may have shifted from communal upliftment to an individualized self-concept with materialism and individualism as its driving force. Consequently, these
realities may distract members of the African American community from the challenges that we face as a race of people.

Therefore, meaningful patterns of communal resistance are
perhaps replaced by the disproportional emphasis of the pursuit
of self-aggrandizement at the individual level. Consumer spending ability has replaced interest and investment in transforma-
tional collective activity as the barometer of how African Americans guage their worth and value in American society (Boyd,
2003). It appears that many of the cultural meanings in Black
society are influenced by this community's uncritical acceptance
of the European worldview, which is lodged in American cultural ethos. The absorption of a non-African worldview seems
to have spawned an anti-African cultural spirit in the African
American community (Ani, 1994). This betrays the ancestral
and collective spirit of past struggle and reduces the possibility
of future advancement of the community of interests located in
the African American experience in America.

This work does not suggest that African Americans exist
in a monolithic shell, with non varying symmetrical realities.
However, this study does acknowledge the actuality that as a community, many times African Americans face similar challenges in
different degrees and gradations because of the lingering effects
of racism, prejudice, bigotry, and discrimination in America and
its major institutions (Myers, 1999; Cashin, 2004). The business

and corporate entities appear to recognize little value in chang-ing the artistic nature of non-conscious rap.

Therefore, it is imperative that African American parents inculcate their children and communities with the African world-view. This is necessary in order to arm African American young people against the debilitating effects of the European world-view, which is located in non-conscious rap and its concurrent major themes and images. The critical socialization and mainte-nance of African worldview can protect African Americans from the uncritical internalization of European worldview and its plausible link to anti-African maladaptive behaviors—many of which are perpetuated in non-conscious rap. Cultural renewal is crucial for the well-being of African Americans as Akoto (1992) asserts: "The interest of Afrikans are best served through the pursuit of self determination as a people. That pursuit begins with the revivification of one's cultural heritage" (p. 80). Early racial socialization of African culture and African worldview will help African American children build their African self-con-sciousness (Sutherland, 1997). This may be useful to neutralize the pervasive messages and images of non-concious rap because of its corollary European worldview influences. Jamison (2006) asserts that, "...a strong ASC may serve as a buffer that limits the amount of exposure to rap lyrics that distort perceptions of Afri-can-American masculinity, and may redirect the interests of Afri-can-American males towards culturally affirmative experiences" (p. 45). Because of its wide acceptance among African American youth non-conscious rap is one of the main "contingencies of reinforcement" (B.F. Skinner, 1969) for European worldview in the millennium. Skinner posits: "A culture is not the behavior of the people "living in it"; it is "it" in which they live—the contin-gencies of social reinforcement which generate and sustain their behavior" (p. 13). This viewpoint is echoed by Abraham (1962) as he argues, "All events of large significance take place within the setting of some culture, and indeed derive their significance from the culture in which they find themselves" (p.11).

The imposition of European worldview has altered the cul-tural "geography of the mind" of African Americans (Skinner, 1969, p. 265). It appears to have moved their social, political, and

economic realities away from the African worldview/ cosmological tenets that are centered on communalism. Consequently,
many African Americans have shifted toward the European
worldview construct that is illuminated in self-concepts based on
individualism, materialism, and competition. This may explain
the discourse surrounding the alleged "nihilism" in African
American communities (West, 1993). The imposition of European worldview continues because it poses as universal and not
particular. Huntington (2003) contends:

> In the nineteenth century the idea of "The white
> man's burden" helped justify the extension of
> Western political and economic domination over
> non-Western societies. At the end of the twentieth
> century the concept of a universal civilization helps
> justify Western cultural dominance of other societ-
> ies and the need for those societies to ape Western
> practices and institutions. (p. 66)

The end result of African Americans' wholesale adoption of
European worldview has observable consequences as Hilliard
(1998) contends: "Many Africans around the world have abandoned African cultural practices and tried to "ape" European
practices" (p. 31). The results of the alien state of nature hypothesis put forth earlier in this work can be seen in the anti-African
practices of some African Americans. West (1992) argues, "This
usually results in a numbing detachment from others and a self-
destructive disposition toward the world" (p. 40).

The power of European worldview and its cultural exten-
sions in America cannot be underestimated, specifically its strong
influences on African Americans. West asserts, "The nihilistic
threat is now more powerful than ever before because the armor
to ward against it is weaker" (p. 41). West illuminates the power
of an alien worldview system on the lives of African Americans.
Its effects are hard to escape unless the person of African descent
is socialized early and grounded in African worldview, which
will lead to a strong sense of African self-consciousness. West
maintains: "The genius of our black foremothers and forefathers
was to create powerful buffers to ward off the nihilistic threat, to

equip folk with cultural armor to beat back the demons of hopelessness, meaninglessness, and lovelessness" (p. 40).

The African worldview construct is the culturally affirmative idea that neutralizes the effects of European worldview on the lives of African Americans, which I maintain is the catalytic basis for the nihilistic threat that West advances but does not critique. Worldview constructs are the prism through which people look to guide and govern their lives in all areas of human activity. Consequently, a worldview should reflect a people's collective history and indigenous culture in order for them to move forward in a state of health. According to Jean (1991), "An African-centered perspective can provide a resource for the creative restructuring of the social order'" (p. xi).

In order for African Americans to thrive as a productive "collective" community in the midst of a proliferation of non-African worldviews, it is essential that they return to the ideas and life practices of their ancestors'. Akoto (1992) maintains:

> We must begin with culture. As a people, the issue of culture is perhaps more important to us than most because of the disruption and the distortion of our history and culture during the course of the two millennia war of conquest against Afrika and the subsequent Holocaust of Afrikan enslavement. (p.193).

Cultural grounding is a vital component of a people's collective well-being. It serves to anchor and guide a common destiny as well as focus its members in a concerted direction. African worldview recognizes the place of the individual. Gyekye (1987) observes, "On the one hand, the value attached to the idea of individual has been so exaggerated in the capitalist system as to detach the person from the natural communal social environment" (p.162). Elements of individuality do exist in the African worldview construct as it is seen through the Akan social system; however, the role of the individual is distinctly different in form and practice from the European model. According to Gyekye, "The individual is supposed to have a dual responsibility: for oneself as an individual as well as to the group" (p.161). In Akan social thought the individual is responsible to the collective and at no time rewarded for individual accomplishments that do not enhance or reflect upon the group's interests. The ideas expressed by Gyekye are in concert with the scholarly understandings put forth by other scholars on the significance of the African world-view to African-Americans (Ani, 1994; Asante, 1998; Azibo, 2001; A.N. Wilson, 1993). The African worldview represents the fundamental values exclusive to the unique and specific collective history of African people dislocated in America. Existing in an alien space presents people of African descent unique and particular challenges because of Anglo-Saxons' historical reactions to their pigmentation.

The African worldview construct re-centers African Americans in a reality that suits their well-being as Asante (1998) asserts:

> Regaining our own platforms, standing in our own cultural spaces, and believing that our way of viewing the universe is just as valid as any, we will achieve the kind of transformation that we need to participate fully in a multicultural society. However, without this kind of centeredness, we bring almost nothing to the multicultural table but a darker version of whiteness. (p. 8)

Asante's position highlights the profound need for African world-view and its clear utility for the well-being of African Americans. The conceptualization of the African worldview construct and orientation is essentially a question of human agency. America has historically been resistant to the notion of African American agency specifically when it is generated through an African-centered paradigm (Ani, 1994; Asante, 1998; Sutherland, 1997).

The subject of agency has always been of vital concern to most people of African descent in America. The denial of their human freedom and the resultant suppression of agency and self-determination place African Americans in a unique position (Bell, 2004; Cone, 1970; Franklin and Moss, 2000). It is because of the history of oppression and white supremacy that is inherent in the American experience that African Americans with a sense of race maintenance have relied upon African worldview to sustain them. According to Loewen (1995), "Perhaps the most pervasive theme in our history is the domination of black America by white America"(p. 31). The domination that Loewen speaks to is centered on the suppression of African Americans' right to agency and self-sovereignty. At the cultural level these realities are enveloped in the imposition of European worldview.

Moving beyond ordinary articles of faith in terms of social ordering, the African worldview construct aligns African Americans with their original state of nature at the most basic levels of existence. This alignment assures the African American community a constant collective trajectory toward communal growth and well-being decentering and destabilizing the paralysis of the individualistic thrust inherent in European worldview. When the clutches of alien worldviews are released, African Americans can operate more focused on the interests of their communities. West (1993) posits:

> What has changed? What went wrong" The bitter irony of integration? The cumulative effects of a genocidal conspiracy? The virtual collapse of rising expectations after the optimistic sixties. None of us fully understands why the cultural structures that once sustained black life are no longer able to fend off the nihilistic threat. (p.15)

Taking strong exception with West's intellectual posture and approach, African-centered theorists (Akbar, 1984; Asante, 1990, 1998, 2003a; Azibo, 2001; Jamison, 2006; Kambon,1992,1998; Myers,1993; Nobles, 2006; Sutherland, 1997) have argued for the redemptive power of the African worldview construct as the way forward for the maintenance of African Americans' collective well-being. The development of critical African self-consciousness is vital for the survival of African Americans in a culture that promotes one worldview (Kambon, 1992).

When African Americans are submerged in an alien world-view construct, the dynamics of their thinking are altered and this affects the collective well-being of this community. African worldview represents the fundamental values that are wedded to the successful survival thrust of African Americans. These precepts are unique and specific to the collective history of African people displaced in America.

Chapter 7

THE DOCTRINE OF WELLNESS OF BEING

African Americans face race-specific challenges when they adopt alien worldviews and operate their lives in great distance from their indigenous African ways of being (Akbar, 1984; Asante, 2002; Baldwin and Hopkins, 1990; Hilliard, 1998; Myers, 1999; Sutherland, 1997; A.N. Wilson, 1993). It also appears that racism and its attendant subcultures: discrimination, prejudice, and bigotry—while reappearing in different forms and practices are as resilient as ever in America and the larger world (Asante, 2003b; Kovel, 1984). Therefore, because of the apparent intractability of these conditions some African Americans must be re-socialized to work in their collective best interests, as other ethnic groups have done and continue to do. According to Clausen (1968), "Socialization may be viewed from the perspective of the individual or from that of a collectivity (be it the larger society or a constituent group) having a distinct subculture" (p. 4).

Pursuant to their historical experiences in America, African Americans are a racialized constituent group. The term "socialization" is used by social scientists to refer to the process of learning one's culture and how to live within it. For individuals it provides the knowledge necessary for living and advancing within their society. For society, socialization is the "means by which social and cultural continuity are attained" (Clausen, 1968, p. 5). The socialization of African Americans by American cultural institutions that are centered on European worldview appears to have caused many African Americans to think of their individual well-being first at the expense of the African American collective. This is cause for concern specifically when examining the major social indices for African-Americans who are consistently at the bottom. These differences display themselves in quality-of-life realities as Winant (2001) contends:

> Pick any relevant sociological indicator—life expectancy, infant mortality, literacy, access to health care, income level—and apply it in virtually any setting, global, regional, or local, and the results will be the same: the worldwide correlation of wealth and well-being with white skin and European descent, and of poverty and immiseration with dark and "otherness." (p. 305)

Racial ideology plays a significant role in Winant's observation and that point is supported in this work and by other researchers (Walters, 2003; A.N. Wilson, 1998; D. Wilson, 2007; W.J. Wilson, 1973; and Wright, 1984).

ECONOMICS AND ALIEN WORLDVIEWS

Scholars also contend that economics is the key to African American equality and freedom (Anderson, 2001; A.N. Wilson, 1998). It is valid to highlight that African Americans have made significant inroads economically, in terms of buying power as evidenced by Humphreys (2007):

> In 2007, African Americans will constitute the nation's largest racial minority market, and their economic clout will energize the U.S. consumer market as never before. The Selig Center projects that the nation's black buying power will rise from $318 billion in 1990 to $590 billion in 2000, to $845 billion in 2007, and to $1.1 trillion in 2012. The

> 1990 to 2007 percentage gain of 166 percent out-
> strips the 124 percent increase in white buying power
> and the 134 percent increase in total buying power
> (all races combined). In 2007, the nation's share of
> total buying power that is black will be 8.4 percent,
> up from 7.4 percent in 1990. African-American con-
> sumers share of the nation's total buying power will
> rise to 8.7 percent in 2012, accounting for almost
> nine cents out of every dollar that is spent. (p. 4)

However, it is equally valid to explore why gross quality-of-
life disparities continue to exist among most African Americans,
in spite of their reported economic potency. I am not confusing
Black buying power with Black net worth, but I do seek to illuminate the collective economic possibilities and potential self-help
power of this group. So therefore a larger question must be considered: Considering their history of collective oppression, why
don't African Americans as a group use their "economic clout"
(Humphreys, 2007, p. 4) to structurally invest in and better the
lives of all African Americans? One explanation may be the lack
of community-and family-based African-centered worldview
socialization in post-civil rights Black America. According to
Myers (1999) a *Belief Systems Analysis* (BSA) is necessary in the
African-American community. Myers (1999) maintains:

> ...BSA was created as a broad-based therapeutic strat-
> egy for restoring health and balance to people whose
> mental health had been impaired by the psychologi-
> cal oppression of a worldview that is antithetical to
> that holistic understanding which can be traced back
> to the wisdom tradition in the beginning of human
> culture and civilization. (p. 328)

The mass application of the BSA in African-American communities may serve as an intervention to address many of the
debilitating effects of alien worldviews that are plaguing this community. Myers (1999) holds, "Utilizing BSA, the first phase of the
therapeutic relationship is geared toward helping the participants
to see the relationship between their current belief systems and

their experiences" (p. 329). This step is vital if African Americans are ever to extricate themselves from the maladaptive behaviors and life practices caused by the complete adoption of alien worldviews. These foreign and exotic ways of being are unable to produce African-centered behaviors that align themselves with the positive survival thrust and communal well-being of people of African descent in America. If African Americans continue to adopt and live within alien worldview constructs, their lives will continue to be aligned with a form of polite slavery, at the level of human functioning. Non-African worldview orientations may cause African Americans to continue to live individualistic, anti-communal existences, which lead to our inability to serve our own interests as a collective. It is plausible to assume that if African Americans continue to be saturated with the European worldview construct, then it will be increasingly difficult for us to think independently outside of Western conceptualizations of ourselves and our communities. What these observations support is the idea that African Americans may be working against their own collective well-being, if they continue to absorb and adopt non-African life practices. African-centered cultural congruency is a vital component of African American health as Cheikh Anta Diop (in B.E. Wright, 1984) explained, "I consider culture as a rampart which protects a people, a collectivity. Culture must above all, play a protective role: It must insure the cohesion of the group" (pp. 30-37).

Living within absolute European worldview domination, African American cohesion is improbable because, as Myers (1993) maintains, "Individualism, competition, and materialism provide criteria for self-definition as a natural consequence of a worldview in which finite and limited focus orients us toward such disorder that we fight one another to sustain an illusion" (p. 10). The adherence to the African worldview construct by African Americans insures that their survival thrust remains communal and is perpetuated as well as maintained in an intergenerational manner.

Clearly, African Americans are in need of an African-centered holistic resource to guide them forward in their struggle for collective meaning and purpose. The wide disparities in all the major social indices between white and Black citizens in the

United States warrants the construction of a wellness plan for African Americans. Looking at this challenge from an African-centered standpoint is necessary, if a forward thinking congruent worldview conceptualization is to be developed for African Americans. Asante (1998) has argued that African Americans have been taken off of their own terms and forced to live in borrowed spaces; this observation resonates in the lived realities of many Black people in America.

AFRICAN TRADITIONAL LIFE PRACTICES

The Doctrine of Wellness of Being seeks to restore order to the chaos of African American life in America. This disorder was caused by the disruption of African belief systems, which began with the period of enslavement and continues with the onslaught and imposition of European worldview in American life. The Doctrine of Wellness of Being is an African traditional life practices system that will reorient African Americans to their original ways of being. This conceptualization suggests that when faced with domination the healthy African person is actively engaged in a state of resistance against domination using the ancestral teachings of African sages from antiquity.

The Doctrine of Wellness of Being is a Sankofan retrieval system designed to refocus and return African Americans back to their original life practices and worldview. This system offers African Americans lessons to live by in a foreign land that has a dominant alien worldview set in place. The major components of this system are chosen because the original authors of the meanings are scribes of the classical African tradition, although modern-day translations will be used in this work. The Doctrine of Wellness of Being is a moral, practical, and ethical guide for African Americans. It consists of three main parts:

1. Maat
2. Nguzo Saba
3. The Husia

This Doctrine of Wellness of Being is beneficial for African Americans because as Carruthers (in Karenga, 1984) argues, "The quest for spiritual enrichment among Black people in the physical and cultural Diaspora has led to the adoption of the Holy Books of other peoples: the Torah, the Bible and the Quran" (p. ix). This work does not suggest that these writings are better or worse for those who choose them, however this study is in agreement with Carruthers when he states, "The fact that Black people could find spiritual comfort in those alien scriptures speaks both to the African contributions to those religions and the intensity of the African spiritual quest" (p. ix). African Americans have a race-specific unique history in America altered by oppression. This reality has in many forms pushed them away from their original states of nature. This is evidenced by their continued acceptance of alien life practices. By utilizing the best practices of African traditions, the Doctrine of Wellness of Being will refocus African Americans in an African-centered direction toward healing and communal growth. The Doctrine of Wellness of Being is centered on the belief that African Americans can find their way forward through the 21st century only by affirming their African ancestral traditions. This is vital if this population is to advance not as individuals, but as a collective entity. This reality has been realized by other ethnic/religious groups in America without the reprisals, second guessing, and charges of "reverse racism" that are levied against African Americans by the larger body politic, whenever this group attempts to serve its own interests.

THE CONCEPTUAL IDEAL OF MAAT

Maat is the first conceptual ideal in the Doctrine of Wellness of Being. Karenga (1990) maintains, "For Maat is the fundamental principle of ancient life. It is the fundamental principle of the divine, natural and social order" (p. 23). In contemporary African American life a public standard for behavior that is based on African ideals is absent as Beatty (2002) contends:

> Maat is a concept that is fundamental in understanding the Kemetic (ancient Egyptian) and hence the

African world view. Embedded in Maat are a number
of critical assumptions about the nature of the cosmos,
society, the person, and their inextricable interrelat-
edness which are in stark contrast and indeed, alien to
the narrative of Western civilization. (p. 212)

However, African Americans are subject to the laws and codes
of conduct that govern America. Obenga (2002) says, a relationship can be drawn between this fact and rulers of the Near
East, "... whose actions were motivated by politics and the will
to control people as opposed to attempting to establish and
maintain harmony, order, and balance" (p. 38). Consequently,
a larger, more meaningful issue is: What are the ethical ideals
that stem from the African tradition that can be actualized in
modern-day America for African Americans considering their
position as a historically oppressed group? Looking at this issue
Karenga (1990) contends, "Maat as rightness in the divine,
natural and social sense becomes the unifying principles of existence" (p. 24). The unifying principles that Karenga illuminates
along with the application of African worldview are the forces
necessary to combat the "nihilism" that West (1993) advances.
Karenga (1990) continues, "...Maat becomes the measurement
of thought, emotion, speech and conduct, and a goal of practice.
But in addition, Maat becomes a reward in itself for it builds
character and community and insures immortality" (pp. 24-25).

The character-building and communal aspect of Maat is critical because it has been established that African Americans have
been moved away from their cultural centers and forced to live
on the borrowed terms of others (Asante, 1998). Maat delivers
African Americans back to their selves in a harmonious order as
Obenga (2002) writes: "The alienation, selfishness, uncertainty,
and disorder that modern man experiences speaks to the fundamental failure to view human possibility in a Maatian sense of
divine order that encompasses the cosmos, the society, and the
individual" (pp. 43-44). African Americans have been put in the
unique position of living an alienated existence. This population,
because of the remnants of the enslavement period, Jim Crow,
legal segregation, and modern-day cultural mis-orientation is

estranged from its indigenous ancestral traditions at the basic levels of human functioning (Eyerman , 2001; Leary, 2005). Historically, this community has been rewarded for the amount of distance it maintains from all things African (Hilliard, 1998).

The Doctrine of Wellness of Being will refocus African Americans on their basic, natural, and ancestral states of nature. When utilized properly, this system will empower African Americans because it helps them to internally redefine their socially constructed identities irrespective of the dominant order. Maat contains seven core principles that determine and reiterate its ideals at the basic level. These components serve as a guide for a structured and ordered African American existence in an alien environment. According to Karenga (1993), "Maat means many things, including truth, justice, propriety, harmony, balance, reciprocity and order--in a word, rightness in the divine, natural and social realms" (p. 86). These principles give African Americans a guidepost to live by in an America that places high value on individualism and material interests. The Doctrine of Wellness of Being seeks to develop among African Americans a common value system located in African ideals that will reduce the divisive polarization produced by self-interest that exists in many segments of this community. This system aims to begin a new "Symbolic Interactionism" (Blumer, 1969) between African-Americans and foster a spirit of mutual cooperation.

THE NGUZO SABA PRINCIPLES

The Nguzo Saba (Karenga, 1997) represents seven practical African principles that ground and center African Americans on ideas that benefit them as a community. It does not speak to individual successes but extols the virtues of communal and collective effort. This is necessary if a linkage is to be made to meaningful practices from the African past, as Akoto (1992) contends: "In establishing that linkage, we must not seek to replicate meaningless customs or structural and behavioral features that are irrelevant or would result in internal conflict, stagnation, or inefficiency" (p. 192). The major components of the Nguzo Saba are practical, relevant, and applicable to the current challenges that African-Americans face in America. In an increasingly indi-vidualized Black America these concepts offer grounding and a singular focus on the reinvigoration of Black collective thought and action. The seven principles are (Karenga, 1997, pp. 5-6):

1. Umoja (Unity): To strive for and maintain unity in the family, community, nation and race.
2. Kujichagulia (Self-Determination): To define ourselves, name ourselves, create for ourselves and speak for ourselves.
3. Ujima (Collective Work and Responsibility): To build and maintain our community together and make our brothers' and sisters' problems our problems and to solve them together.
4. Ujamaa (Cooperative Economics): To build and main-tain our own stores, shops and other businesses and to profit from them together.
5. Nia (Purpose): To make our collective vocation the building and developing of our community in order to restore our people to their traditional greatness.
6. Kuumba (Creativity): To do always as much as we can, in the way we can, in order to leave our community more beautiful and beneficial than we inherited it.
7. Imani (Faith): To believe with all our heart in our people, our parents, our teachers, our leaders and the righteous-ness and victory of our struggle.

The Nguzo Saba serves as a guide of practical meanings to remind African Americans of their ancestral responsibility to think in terms of the well-being of the community, versus the individualized self. The Doctrine of Wellness of Being does not propose a racialized separatist agenda. However, it is focused on the well-being of African Americans, because of this communi-ty's unique relationship with historical campaigns of structured inequality, which have produced the observable disparities that exist in the major quality-of-life indicators measured in America. The history of American racism has produced a particular trauma that many African Americans experience. As a result this population has been engaged in an ongoing battle against what Eyerman (2004) defined as "cultural trauma: "Cultural trauma refers to a dramatic loss of identity and meaning, a tear in the social fabric, affecting a group of people that has achieved some degree of cohesion" (p. 61). The loss of African identity is demonstrated in the fragmentation, chaos, individualism, and lack of group focus present in many Black communities in the United States. African Americans must be refocused on our African cultural elements. The instructive narrative of Clough (1960) for Americans of European descent is also useful for African Americans regarding their African cultural values. Clough maintains, "It is important for all of us to be clear regarding our values that we do not take a vague or uncritical attitude toward them, nor by too great familiarity with them to realize their true worth" (p .4).

Moral realities are a part of the African American question as well as their connection to an African moral code. When these are not connected to African reality, problems may arise as Nobles, Lawford, and Cavil (1985) observe: "When the moral demand and the symbolic systems lose their legitimacy and the power to compel thought and action, then disruption occurs in the culture, growth and development cease and the behavior of the people become aberrant and dysfunctional" (p. 5). The chaotic nature of many African American communities may be related to the lack of an African moral/ethical system required to balance the disproportionate imposition of the European worldview construct. A consistent African American ethos or set of guiding principles would help to offset this imbalance.

THE HUSIA AND WISE INSTRUCTION

The Husia explicates the ancient Egyptian sacred wisdoms. This body of knowledge contains books of wise instruction by the African ancients. The Husia is not offered here as a replacement for whatever spiritual system one practices nor is it being positioned as better or worse than any. The Husia's basic principles are not driven by denominational restraints. The Husia and all the elements of the Doctrine of Wellness of Being can supplement all religious systems practiced by African Americans. However, it is being argued here that the teachings in the Husia (although translated) reflect an original and authentic system of beliefs authored by African people (Karenga, 1984; Nobles, Lawford, & Cavil, 1985). The Husia through its "Books of Wise Instruction" (Karenga, 1984) shows a path and orients African Americans towards ancient ideas on how to live a life. Karenga (1984) contends:

> The Books of Wise Instruction are as sacred as any of the other books of the Husia, for the main focus is on maat and the moral and spiritual obligation each person has in preserving and practicing it in and for the community. (p. 39)

Utilizing the ancient wisdoms found in the Husia gives African Americans a centralized focus on intra-cultural behavior and reduces the intra-racial conflict that impedes concerted, collective efforts toward the communal well-being of this community

The Doctrine of Wellness of Being is a conceptual model designed to reorient African-Americans toward their ancestral ways of being. It is necessary because of the infusion of alien values in the African world. As a conceptual model this system seeks to develop two kinds of positive behavioral functionalities for African Americans:

1. The Optimal Functioning Individual (Myers, 1999).
2. The Authentic Struggler (Sutherland, 1997).

According to Myers (1999) the characteristics of the Optimal Functioning Individual (OFI) are:

a. Embraces the higher consciousness of truth, justice, harmony, balance and order.
b. Works to overcome his/her lower nature, rebuking jealousy, envy, greed, and wanton self-interest.
c. Careful to insure that his/her good is not defined by his/her senses.
d. Is free thinking and avoids getting caught up in the illusions of others (pp. 326-327).

In terms of individual differences in response to the struggle for liberation for African Americans, Sutherland (1997) defines the "authentic struggler" as:

> The authentic struggler accepts that the liberation of the oppressed is facilitated when, at the individual level, the person of African descent sees value in self. Thus the authentic struggler is dedicated to his or her African self and by extension to all African persons. Behavioral manifestations of this level of dedication involves not allowing the oppressor to manipulate him or her to maintain the oppression of people of African descent. The authentic struggler lives in accordance with African-centered attitudes, and places great value on the interconnectedness of African people. (p. 58)

The resulting behavioral modifications sought by this wellness model will facilitate a renewed interest in the collective efforts to resolve many of the issues facing the African American community. This model will produce a spirit of self-determining, self-defining, independent self-help strategies that would rely on the internal resources of African Americans. These strategies would free this community from the criticisms of dependency that have plagued and neutralized their most valid calls for structural, systemic, and institutional assistance. As Hilliard (1998) observes, "Once we see ourselves from our own cultural and ethnic base, we will be more cohesive, trusting of each other, and capable of mobilizing to promote our welfare globally" (p. 31).

The Doctrine of Wellness of Being is an African-based systematic positive retrieval of African principles that have relevance in today's world for African Americans. The Doctrine of Wellness of Being is designed to refocus African Americans on their ancestral cultural truths so that this community may collectively prosper and reestablish its communal links to each other in America and the world.

Conclusions

In this work I investigated the ideological elements of domination that have influenced African Americans from 1980 to 2007. Setting about this task required an understanding that most African Americans are not on an equal footing with other groups in terms of the prevailing quality-of-life indicators in America. Specific focus was placed on ideological formations and positions that if accepted uncritically by African Americans, will continue to maintain position and privilege for other groups.

Political stances predicated on racialized ideological subjectivities were examined and exposed for their production of disparate outcomes for African Americans. I explored the fundamental precepts located in the radical conservative political position and exposed its primary objectives and motives in terms of domination. I also revealed the objectives of the neoliberal project and discovered very nuanced but profound denials of African agency in many of its ideological platforms. I assessed the efficacy of popular rhetorical stances as they relate to domination and determined if these ideas advance the agency of African Americans.

In this work I systematically investigated the influence of the European worldview construct on African Americans and determined that it contains elements that do not fully serve the collective and communal interests of African Americans. By looking closely at the ideas that are embedded in the operational ethos of American culture, I was able to conclude that it is vital that African Americans retain a cultural linkage to their African indigenous ways of being in order for them to advance collectively and move forward communally in the diaspora.

The findings of this work suggest that many of the challenges that African Americans collectively face are a result of this population being culturally distanced from their original African states of nature. The resultant influence from the imposition of an alien worldview paradigm on African Americans has led many in this population to engage in behaviors that reflect the values located in non-African worldview absorption.

This works' development of newly operationalized terms such as Agency Reduction Formations and the Post-Racial Project offer African Americans and all members of the human family a new nomenclature and definitional lens to make informed decisions. This work examines the ideological positions that seek to influence the lives of African Americans and also exposes the measureable outcomes that go unchanged as a result of these ideas.

This work investigated the racialization of poverty and the corollary criminal status that was given to impoverished African American aid recipients by the conservative project. This knowledge is vital if an understanding of present racial realities concerning welfare reform is to be understood from a position of balance and objectivity. Conclusively, I maintain that neoliberal and neoconservative welfare reforms are not prescriptive but punitive and ultimately reduce the potential human agency of poor African Americans disproportionately based on race and gender.

The rhetorical formations that I identified in this work and located in the Post- Racial Project have shown themselves to have little utility for African Americans when they are examined from a material perspective. Additionally, these ideas were shown to have minimal effect on the political economy as it pertains to African Americans at the institutional and systemic levels. This work found that the corpus of ideas located in the Post-Racial Project distracts Americans from the real issues surrounding domination and in the final analysis acts as a buffer to conceal material and economic truths. This study points out the reality that if African Americans in a wholesale fashion uncritically accept these positions and make important life choice and legislative decisions based on the hidden agendas of these ideas, this population will continue to be marginalized in terms of advancement and collective agency.

This study investigated the dichotomous worldview constructs that exist between Africans and Europeans. The analysis revealed that African Americans are best served by adhering to their original indigenous African worldview paradigms. This position is advanced through the study's state-of-nature hypothesis. This was done by examining African American activity related to spirituality, culture, and behavioral functioning. In the worldview analysis chapter I demonstrated the need for African Americans to return to the original sources that sustained this population through periods of profound injustice such as: enslavement, Jim Crow, and legally sanctioned segregation in America. The remnants of these time periods are still alive today for African Americans albeit in different structural forms and institutional outcomes.

Last, through detailed investigation I discovered a need for a holistic program of instruction and guidance for African Americans. Based on African principles the development of the Doctrine of Wellness of Being serves as a holistic resource for this population to turn to that speaks to African principles and ways of life. This Sankofan retrieval system re-roots African Americans and serves as protection against the imposition of alien, foreign, and exotic states of nature prevalent in African American life.

I went about this work as a mercenary of an emancipating vision for African Americans. So often we are left out in the world of ideas in ways that can benefit our overall well-being. Whether we are in the south or west side of Chicago, Illinois, the 3rd or 5th ward in Houston, Texas, the west side of Louisville, Kentucky, in Flint, Michigan, the 9th ward of New Orleans Louisiana, the west side of Philadelphia, Pennsylvania or the streets of East Oakland, California, we often find ourselves vulnerable to ideas that blame us for the totality of our conditions. This ahistorical ideological assault by anti-egalitarian loyalists, has worked its way into our national psyche with devastating consequences. While it is meaningful to see how far we have come it is equally valid to spend time examining the obstacles that prevent all of us from moving forward in a collective fashion. While others critique our circumstances and see us as a people on the brink of extinction, I see us as a family poised and thirsty for meaningful information that can allow us to see our reality clearly, take stock, and advance. When looking at our lived realities it is easy to see a long road ahead, but that road could not have been any longer than the one our ancestors had taken on our behalf. From 1980 until now our collective efforts have stalled but time again is here for us to regain our communal position, remember our love for each other, and embrace the ancestral traditions that held our communities intact during the harshest of times. People of African descent don't need any more stars in the public sphere to tell us their "personal opinions"; we need African-centered research that provides useful information so we can make informed decisions. This work is my contribution to that effort, unapologetically ... and may the Ancestors be pleased.

Appendix A

Distribution of AFDC Families by Race of Parent
1983 – 1996

Fiscal Year	Race of Parent					
	White	African-American	Hispanic	Asian	Native-American	Unknown
1983...........	36.5	38.3	10.5	1.3	0.9	12.6
1984...........	36.6	36.7	10.7	1.8	0.9	3.9
1985...........	40.8	41.6	13.6	2.4	1.2	2.2
1986...........	39.7	40.7	14.4	2.3	1.3	1.4
1987...........	38.8	39.8	15.5	2.6	1.3	2.0
1988...........	38.8	39.8	15.7	2.4	1.4	1.9
1989...........	38.4	40.1	15.9	2.7	1.3	1.5
1990...........	38.1	39.7	16.6	2.8	1.3	1.5
1991...........	38.1	38.8	17.4	2.8	1.3	1.6
1992...........	38.9	37.2	17.8	2.8	1.4	2.0
1993...........	38.3	36.6	18.5	2.9	1.3	2.2
1994...........	37.4	36.4	19.9	2.9	1.3	2.1
1995...........	35.6	37.2	20.7	3.0	1.3	2.2
1996...........	35.9	37.2	20.7	3.0	1.3	2.2

Source: Department of Health & Human Services, Administration for Children and Families, Office of Family Assistance, *Characteristics and Financial Circumstances of AFDC Recipients, 1996,* and earlier reports.

Appendix B

	Race of Child					
Fiscal Year	White	African-American	Hispanic	Asian	Native-American	Unknown
1983..........	33.7	40.9	12.6	1.8	1.1	9.9
1984..........	34.1	40.4	13.0	2.3	1.1	9.2
1985..........	34.6	41.9	14.5	2.9	1.1	5.0
1986..........	35.1	42.0	15.6	3.1	1.3	3.0
1987..........	34.4	41.1	16.9	3.4	1.3	3.0
1988..........	33.8	41.3	17.4	2.9	1.3	3.2
1989..........	33.5	41.4	17.1	3.8	1.3	2.9
1990..........	33.1	41.4	17.7	3.9	1.3	2.7
1991..........	33.5	40.1	18.5	3.7	1.3	2.9
1992..........	33.9	38.5	18.7	3.9	1.6	3.4
1993..........	33.7	38.0	19.5	3.8	1.4	3.7
1994..........	33.0	37.9	21.2	3.6	1.4	2.9
1995..........	31.2	38.5	22.2	4.1	1.5	2.4
1996..........	31.6	38.4	22.4	3.8	1.4	2.4

Source: Department of Health & Human Services, Administration for Children and Families, Office of Family Assistance, *Characteristics and Financial Circumstances of AFDC Recipients, 1996*, and other reports.

References

Abraham, M. (2006). Supreme rhetoric: The Supreme Court, veiled majoritarianism, and the enforcement of the racial contract. In J. Young & J.E. Braziel (Eds.), *Race and the foundations of knowledge: Cultural amnesia in the Academy* (pp. 63-74). Urbana, IL: University of Illinois Press.

Abraham, W.E. (1962). *The mind of Africa.* Chicago: The University of Chicago Press.

Akbar, N. (1984). *Chains and images of psychological slavery.* Jersey City, NJ: New Mind Productions.

Akbar, N. (2008). *Dr. Na'im Akbar.* Retrieved January 21, 2008, from http://www.naimakbar.com/index.cfm?pageId=3.

Akoto, K.A. (1992). *Nation building: Theory and practice in Afrikan centered education.* Washington, DC: Pan Afrikan World Institute.

Allimadi, M. (2002). *The Hearts of darkness: How white writers created the racist image of Africa.* New York: Black Star Books.

Anderson, C. (2001). *PowerNomics: The national plan to empower black America.* Bethesda, MD: PowerNomics Corporation of America.

Andreasen, R.O. (2000). Race: Biological reality or social construct? *Philosophy of Science, 67*(3), S653-S667.

Ani, M. (1994). *Yurugu: An African-centered critique of European cultural thought and behavior.* Trenton, NJ: Africa World Press.

Appiah, K.A. (1992). *In my father's house: Africa in the philosophy of culutre.* New York: Oxford University Press.

Appiah, K.A. & Gutmann A. (1996). *Color conscious: The political morality of race.* Princeton, NJ: Princeton University Press.

Asante, M.K. (1990). *Kemet, Afrocentricity and knowledge.* Trenton, NJ: Africa World Press.

Asante, M.K. (1998). *The Afrocentric idea* (rev. ed.). Philadelphia: Temple University Press.

Asante, M.K. (1999). *The painful demise of eurocentrism: An Afrocentric response to critics.* Trenton, NJ: Africa World Press.

Asante, M.K. (2002). Afrocentricity and the decline of western hegemonic thought: A critique of eurocentric theory and practice. In M. Christian (Ed.), *Black identity in the 20th century: Expressions of the US and UK African Diaspora* (pp. 102-118). London: Hansib Publications Limited.

Asante, M.K. (2003a). *Afrocentricity: The theory of social change* (rev. ed.). Chicago: African American Images.

Asante, M.K. (2003b). *Erasing Racism: The survival of the American Nation.* Amherst, NY: Prometheus Books.

Asante, M.K. (2005). *Race, rhetoric, & identity: The architecton of soul.* Amherst, NY: Humanity Books.

Asante, M.K. (2006). Afrocentricity and the Eurocentric hegemony of knowledge: Contradictions of place. In J. Young & J.E. Braziel (Eds.), *Race and the foundations of knowledge: Cultural amnesia in the Academy* (pp. 145-154). Urbana, IL: University of Illinois Press.

Azibo, D.A. (2001). *Liberation psychology: An introduction to the African personality construct.* Grambling, LA: Grambling State University.

Baldwin, J. (1993). *The fire next time.* New York: Vintage Books.

Baldwin, J.A. (1980). The psychology of oppression. In M.K. Asante & A. Vandi (Eds.), *Contemporary black thought: Alternative analyses in social and behavioral science* (pp. 95-110). Beverly Hills, CA: Sage Publishers.

Baldwin, J.A. (1985). Psychological aspects of European cosmology in American society. *The Western Journal of Black Studies, 9*(4), 216-223.

Baldwin, J.A., & Hopkins, R. (1990). African-American and European-American cultural differences as assessed by the worldviews paradigm: An empirical analysis. *The Western Journal of Black Studies, 14*(1), 38-52.

Bane, M.J., & Ellwood, D.T. (1994). *Welfare realities: From rhetoric to reform.* Cambridge, MA: Harvard University Press.

Barker, L.J., Jones, M.H., & Tate, K. (1999). *African Americans and the American political system* (4th ed.). Upper Saddle River, NJ: Prentice Hall.

Barrett, S.R. (2002). *Culture meets power.* Westport, CT: Praeger.

Beard, C.A. (1986). *An economic interpretation of the Constitution of the United States.* New York: The Free Press.

Beatty, M.H. (2002). Maat: The cultural and intellectual allegiance of a concept. In J.H. Carruthers & L.C. Harris (Eds.), *African world history project: The preliminary challenge* (pp. 211-244). Los Angeles: Association for the Study of Classical African Civilizations.

Bell, D. (2004). *Silent covenants: Brown v. Board of Education and the unfilled hopes for racial reform.* New York: Oxford University Press.

Bennett, L., Jr. (1961). *Before the Mayflower: A history of black America* (6th ed.). New York: Penguin Books.

Billingsley, A. (1999). *Mighty like a river: The Black church and social reform.* New York: Oxford University Press.

Black, D. (1976). *The behavior of law.* San Diego, CA: Academic Press.

Blumer, H. (1969). *Symbolic Interactionism: Perspective and method.* Englewood Cliffs, NJ: Prentice Hall.

Bonilla-Silva, E. (2001). *White supremacy & racism in the Post-Civil Rights era.* Boulder, CO: Lynne Rienner Publishers.

Bonilla-Silva, E. (2003). *Racism without racists: Color-blind racism and the persistence of racial inequality in the United States.* New York: Rowman & Littlefield.

Boyd, T. (2003). *The New H.N.I.C.: The death of Civil Rights and the reign of hip hop.* New York: New York University Press.

Brown, M.K., Carnoy, M., Currie, E., Duster, T., Oppenheimer, D.B., Shultz, M.M., & Wellman, D. (2003). *Whitewashing race: The myth of a color-blind society.* Los Angeles: University of California Press.

Buchanan, P.J. (2002). *The death of the West: How dying populations and immigrant invasions imperil our country and civilization.* New York: St Martin's Press.

Burrow, R., Jr. (2006). *God and human dignity: The personalism, theology, and ethics of Martin Luther King, Jr.* Notre Dame, IN: University of Notre Dame Press.

Califano, J.A., Jr. (1999, October). What was really great about the great society: The truth behind the conservative myths. *The Washington Monthly, 31,* 13-19.

Callinicos, A. (1990). *Against postmodernism.* New York: St. Martin's Press.

Carr, L.G. (1997). *"Color-Blind" racism.* Thousand Oaks, CA: Sage Publications.

Carter, S.L. (1991). *Reflections of an affirmative action baby.* New York: Basic Books.

Cashin, S. (2004). *The failures of integration: How race and class are undermining the American dream.* New York: PublicAffairs.

Chafe, W.H., Gavins, R., Korstad, Ortiz, P., Parrish, R., Ritterhouse, J., Roberts, K., & Waligora-Davis, N. (2001). *Remembering Jim Crow: African Americans tell about life in the segregated South.* New York: The New Press.

Chew, C. (2006, August 10). Welfare-to-work proposal would limit vocational training. *Diverse: Issues in Higher Education, 23,* 15.

Choi, J.M (1997). Racist ontology, inferiorization, and assimilation. In E.M. Kramer (Ed.), *Postmodernism and race* (pp. 115-127). Westport, CT: Praeger.

Clarke, J.H. (1991). *Notes for an African world revolution: Africans at the crossroads.* Trenton: Africa World Press.

Clausen, J.A. (1968). Socialization as a concept and as a field of study. In J.A. Clausen (Ed.), *Socialization and Society* (pp. 3-17). Boston: Little, Brown and Company.

Clough, S.B. (1960). *Basic values of western civilization.* New York: Columbia Universtiy Press.

Cole, A.M. (2007). *The cult of true victimhood: From the War on Welfare to the War on Terror.* Stanford, CA: Stanford University Press.

Cone, J.H. (1969). *Black theology and black power.* New York: Seabury Press.

Cone, J.H. (1970). *A black theology of liberation.* Philadelphia: JB Lippincott Company.

Cone, J.H. (1975). *God of the oppressed.* New York: The Seabury Press.

Cone, J.H. (1984). *For my people.* Maryknoll, NY: Orbis Books.

Cone, J.H. (1986). *Speaking the truth: Ecumenism, liberation, and black theology.* Grand Rapids: Wm. B. Eerdmans Publishing.

Cone, J.H. (1999). *Risks of Faith.* Boston: Beacon Press.

Connerly, W. (2000). *Creating equal: My fight against race preferences.* San Francisco: Encounter Books.

Coombs, N. (1972). *The black experience in America.* New York: Twayne Publishers.

Cummings, J.F. (2005). *How to rule the world: Lessons in conquest for the modern prince.* Tokyo: Blue Ocean Press.

Davidson, B. (1969). *The African Genius: An introduction to African cultural and social history.* Boston: Little, Brown and Company.

Delgado, R. (1996). *The coming race war?: And other apocalyptic tales of America after Affirmative Action and welfare.* New York: New York University Press.

Department of Health and Human Services (1998, June). *Aid to families with dependent children: The baseline.* Retrieved October 18, 2007 from Department of Health and Human Services Web site http://aspe.hhs.gov/hsp/afdc/afdcbase98exhib.htm.

Dershowitz, A.M. (1994). *The abuse excuse and other cop outs, sob stories and evasions of responsibility.* Boston: Little, Brown & Company.

Diop, C.A. (1974). *The African origin of civilization: Myth or reality.* Chicago: Lawrence Hill Books.

Diop, C.A. (1989). *The cultural unity of black Africa: The domains of matriarchy & of patirarchy in classical anitquity.* London: Karnak House.

D'Souza, D. (1991). *Illiberal education: The politics of race and sex on campus.* New York: The Free Press.

DuBois, W.E.B. (1994). *The souls of black folk.* New York: Dover Publications.

Dyson, M.E. (2003). *Open Mike: Reflections on philosophy, race, sex, culture and religion.* New York: Basic Books.

Eagleton, T. (1996). *The illusions of postmodernism.* Cambridge, MA: Blackwell Publishers.

Economist, (2006). A blunt instrument, *381,* 40.

Edsall, T., & Edsall, M.D. (1992). *Chain reaction: The impact of race, rights, and taxes on American politics.* New York: W.W. Norton & Company.

Elder, L. (2000). *The ten things you can't say in America.* New York: St. Martin's Press.

Eyerman, R. (2001). *Cultural trauma: Slavery and the formation of African American identity.* Cambridge, MA: Cambridge University Press.

Eyerman, R. (2004). Cultural trauma: Slavery and the formation of African American identity. In J.C. Alexander, R. Eyerman, B. Giesen, N.J. Smelser, & P. Sztompka (Eds.), *Cultural trauma and collective identity* (pp. 60-111). Los Angeles: University of California Press.

Fanon, F. (1967). *Black skin, white masks.* New York: Grove Press.

Farmer, B.R. (2006). *American political ideologies: An introduction to the major systems of thought in the 21st Century.* Jefferson, NC: McFarland & Company.

Fernando, S.H., Jr. (1994). *The New Beats: Exploring the music, culture, and attitudes of Hip-Hop.* New York: Doubleday.

Fiske, J. (1996). *Media matters: Race and gender in U.S. politics* (rev. ed.). Minneapolis: University of Minnesota Press.

Fletcher, M. A. (2006, June 29). U.S. moves to get states to put more welfare recipients in work or in training. *The Washington Post,* pp. A02.

Foner, E., & Mahoney, O. (1995). *America's reconstruction: People and politics after the Civil War.* Baton Rouge: Louisiana State University Press.

Fording, R.C. (2006). "Laboratories of Democracy" or symbolic politics?: The racial origins of welfare reform. In S.F. Schram, J. Soss, & R.C. Fording (Eds.), *Race and the politics of welfare reform* (pp. 72-97). Ann Arbor: University of Michigan Press.

Francis, D. R. (2006, August 21). Two cheers for welfare reform. *The Christian Science Monitor*, pp. 17.

Franklin, J.H., & Moss, A.A., Jr. (2000). *From slavery to freedom: A history of African Americans* (8th ed.). Boston: McGraw Hill.

Franklin, R.M. (1997). *Another day's journey: Black churches confronting the American crisis.* Minneapolis: Fortress Press.

Frazier, E.F. (1939). *The negro family in the United States.* Chicago: The University of Chicago Press.

Frazier, E.F. (1957). *The Negro in the United States* (rev. ed.). New York: Macmillan.

Freedman, H.A. (2002). The welfare advocate's challenge: Fighting historic racism in the new welfare system. *Journal of Poverty Law and Policy, May-June,* 31- 38.

Gabriel, J. (1998). *Whitewash: Racialized politics and the media.* London: Routledge.

Garrett, M. (2005). *The Enduring revolution: How the contract with America continues to shape the nation.* New York: Crown Forum.

Gates, H.L., Jr., & West, C. (1996). *The future of the race.* New York: Alfred A Knopf.

Gilens, M. (1999). *Why Americans hate welfare: Race, media, and the politics of antipoverty policy.* Chicago: The University of Chicago Press.

Gillespie, E., & Schellhas, B. (1994). *Contract with America: The bold plan by Rep. Newt Gingrich, Rep. Dick Armey and the House Republicans to change the nation.* New York: Times Books.

Gilroy, P. (2000). *Against race: Imagining political culture beyond the color line.* Cambridge, MA: The Belknap Press of Harvard University Press.

Gimpel, J.G. (1996). *Legislating the revolution: The contract with America in its first 100 days.* Boston: Allyn and Bacon.

Goldberg, D.T. (1993). *Racist Culture: Philosophy and the politics of meaning.* Cambridge, MA: Blackwell.

Gonzales, M.G., & Delgado, R. (2006). *The politics of fear: How Republicans use money, race, and the media to win.* Boulder, CO: Paradigm Publishers.

Gordon, L.R. (1997). *Her majesty's other children: Sketches of racism from a neocolonial age.* New York: Roman and Littlefield.

Gossett, T.F. (1963). *Race: The history of an idea in America.* New York: Oxford University Press.

Gotanda, N. (1991). A critique of "Our Constitution Is Color-Blind". *Stanford Law Review, 44*(1), 1-68.

Gould, S.J. (1996). *The mismeasure of man* (rev. ed.). New York: W W Norton & Company.

Grogger, J., Karoly, L.A., & Klerman, J.A. (2002, July). *Consequences of welfare reform: A research synthesis.* Retrieved November 11, 2007, from U.S. Department of Health and Human Services Web site: http://www.acf.hhs.gov/programs/opre/welfare_employ/res_systhesis/reports/ consequences_of_wr/rand_report.pdf

Gutmann, A. (1995). *Responding to racial injustice: The Tanner lectures on human values.* Retrieved September 12, 2010 from, http://www.tannerlectures.utah.edu/lectures/documents/Gutmann96.pdf

Gyekye, K. (1987). *An essay on African philosophical thought: The Akan conceptual scheme.* New York: Cambridge University Press.

Hacker, A. (1992). *Two nations: Black and white, separate, hostile, unequal* (expanded and updated). New York: Ballantine Books.

Hanchard, M. (2006). *Party politics: Horizons in black political thought.* New York: Oxford University Press.

Haney-Lopez, I. (2006). *White by law: The legal construction of race* (rev. ed. and updated). New York: New York University Press.

Harrell, C.J. (1999). *Manichean psychology: Racism and the minds of people of African descent.* Washington, DC: Howard University Press.

Harris, H. (1997). Growing in glory. *Emerge Magazine, April,* 49-53.

Harris, L. (1995). Postmodernism and utopia, an unholy alliance. In F.L. Hord & J.S. Lee (Eds.), *I am because we are: Readings in black philosophy* (pp. 367- 382). Amherst: University of Massachusetts Press.

Haskins, R. (2006). *Work over welfare: The inside story of the 1996 Welfare Reform Law.* Washington, DC: Brookings Institution Press.

References

Herring, C. & Amissah, C. (1997). Advance and retreat: Racially based attitudes and public policy. In S.A. Tuch & J.K. Martin (Eds.), *Racial attitudes in the 1990s: Continuity and change* (pp. 121-143). Westport, CT: Praeger.

Herrnstein, R.J. & Murray, C. (1994). *The bell curve: Intelligence and class structure in American life.* New York: The Free Press.

Herskovits, M.J. (1941). *The myth of the negro past.* Boston: Beacon Press.

Hill Collins, P. (1990). *Black feminist thought: Knowledge, consciousness, and the politics of empowerment* (Perspectives on Gender, vol. 2). New York: Routledge.

Hilliard, A.G., III (1998). *SBA: The reawakening of the African mind.* Gainesville, FL: Makare Publishing.

Hofstadter, R. (1955). *Social Darwinism in American thought.* Boston: Beacon Press.

Holmes, O.W. (1991). *The common law.* New York: Dover Publications.

Hughes, R. (1993). *Culture of complaint: The fraying of America.* New York: Oxford University Press.

Humphreys, J.M. (2007). The muliticultural economy 2007. *Georgia Business and Economic Conditions, 67*(3), 1-15.

Huntington, S.P. (2003). *The clash of civilizations and the remaking of world order.* New York: Simon & Schuster.

Isaacs, H.R. (1975). *Idols of the tribe: group identity and political change.* New York: Harper & Row.

Isaacs, J.B. (2007). *Economic Mobility of Black and White Families.* Retrieved November 17, 2007, from http://www.pewtrusts.org/uploadedFiles/wwwpewtrustsorg/Reports/Economic-Mobility/EMP%20Black%20and%20White%20Families%20ES+Chapter.pdf.

Jackson, D. Z. (2006, March 1). Halliburton strikes again. *The Boston Globe,* p. A11.

Jackson, J.P., & Weidman, N.M. (2004). *Race, racism, and science: Social impact and interaction.* Santa Barbara, CA: ABC-CLIO.

Jamison, D.F. (2006). The relationship between African self-concious-ness, cultural misorientation, hypermasculinity, and rap music preference. *Journal of African American Studies, 9*(4), 45-60.

Jansson, B.S., & Smith, S. (1996). Articulating a "New Nationalism" in American social policy. *Journal of the National Association of Social Workers, 41*(5), 441-451.

Jean, C.M. (1991). *Behind the Eurocentric veils: The search for African realities.* Amherst: University of Massachusetts Press.

Jewell, K.S. (1993). *From Mammy to Miss America and beyond: cultural images and the shaping of U.S. Social Policy.* London: Routledge.

Jones, J.M. (1972). *Prejudice and racism.* Menlo Park, CA: Addison-Wesley.

Jones, W.R. (1973). *Is God a white racist?: A preamble to Black theology.* Garden City, NY: Anchor Press/Doubleday.

Jost, J.T. & Benaji, M.R. (1994). The role of stereotyping in system-justification and the production of false consciousness. *British Journal of Social Psychology, 33,* 1-27.

Jussim, L., Nelson, T., Manis, M., & Soffin, S. (1995). Prejudice, stereo-types, and labeling effects: Sources of bias in person perception. *Journal of Personality and Social Psychology, 68*(2), 228-246.

Juster, F.T. (1982). The economics and politics of the supply-side view. In T.J. Hailstones (Ed.), *Viewpoints on supply-side economics* (pp. 95-101). Reston, VA: Reston Publishing Company.

Kambon, K.K. (1992). *The African personality in America: An African-centered framework.* Tallahassee, FL: Nubian Nation Publications.

Kambon, K.K.. (1998). *African/Black psychology in the American context: An African-centered approach.* Tallahassee, FL: Nubian Nation Publications.

Kardiner, A., M.D., & Ovesey, L., M.D. (1951). *The mark of oppression: Explorations in the personality of the American Negro.* New York: Meridian Books.

Karenga, M. (1984). *Selections from the Husia: Sacred wisdom of Ancient Egypt.* Los Angeles: The University of Sankore Press.

Karenga, M. (1990). *The book of coming forth by day: The ethics of the Declarations of Innocence.* Los Angeles: University of Sankore Press.

References

Karenga, M. (1993). *Introduction to black studies* (2nd ed.). Los Angeles: University of Sankore Press.

Karenga, M. (1997). *Kwanzaa: A celebration of family, community and culture*. Los Angeles: University of Sankore Press.

Karenga, M. (1999). *Odù Ifá: The ethical teachings*. Los Angeles: University of Sankore Press.

Kennedy, S. (1959). *Jim Crow guide to the U.S.A.: The laws, customs and etiquette governing the conduct of nonwhites and other minorities as second-class citizens*. London: Lawrence & Wishart.

Keyes, A. (1995). *Masters of the dream: The strength and betrayal of Black America*. New York: William Morrow and Company.

Killian, L.M. (1968). *The impossible revolution?: Black power and the American dream*. New York: Random House.

Kitwana, B. (1994). *The rap on gangsta rap: Who run it?: Gangsta rap and visions of black violence*. Chicago: Third World Press.

Knox, R. (1850). *The races of men: A fragment*. London: H Renshaw.

Kovel, J. (1984). *White racism: A psychohistory*. New York: Columbia University Press.

Kull, A. (1992). *The color-blind Constitution*. Cambridge, MA: Harvard University Press.

Leary, J.D. (2005). *Post traumatic slave syndrome: America's legacy of enduring injury and healing*. Milwaukie, OR: Uptone Press.

Lens, V. (2002). TANF: What went wrong and what to do next. *Journal of the National Association of Social Workers, 47*(3), 279-290.

Lewis, L. (2008). Transcending the grosser physical differences of race in contemporary society: An introduction. In L. Lewis & G. Griffith (Eds.), *Color, hair, and bone: Race in the twenty-first century* (pp. 11-28). Cranbury, NJ: Lewisburg Bucknell University Press.

Lieberman, R.C. (1998). *Shifting the color line: Race and the American welfare state*. Cambridge, MA: Harvard University Press.

Lincoln, C.E. (1974). *The black experience in religion*. Garden City, NY: Anchor Press/Doubleday.

Lincoln, C.E. (1978). Black sects and cults and public policy. In J.R. Washington, Jr. (Ed.), *Black religion and public policy: Ethical and historical perspectives* (pp. 1-9). [S.I. : s.n], 1978 .

Lind, M. (1996). *The next American nation: The new nationalism and the fourth American Revolution*. New York: Simon & Schuster.

Loewen, J.W. (1995). *Lies my teacher told me: Everything your American history textbook got wrong*. New York: The New Press.

Loury, G.C. (2002). *The anatomy of racial inequality*. Cambridge, MA: Harvard University Press.

Lurie, I. (2006). *At the front lines of the welfare system: A perspective on the decline in welfare caseloads*. Albany, NY: The Rockefeller Institute Press.

Lyotard, J.F. (1984). *The postmodern condition: A report on knowledge*. Minneapolis: University of Minnesota Press.

Majors, R. & Mancini Bilson, J. (1992). *Cool pose: The dilemas of black manhood in America*. New York: Lexington Books.

Marable, M. (1995). *Beyond black and white: Transforming African-American politics*. London: Verso.

Marable, M. (1997). *Black liberation in conservative America*. Boston: South End Press.

Marable, M. (2000a). Beyond racial identity politics: Towards a liberation theory for multicultural Democracy. In R. Delgado & J. Stefancic (Eds.), *Critical race theory: The cutting edge* (pp. 448-454). Philadelphia: Temple University Press.

Marable, M. (2000b). *How capitalism underdeveloped Black America* (updated ed.). Cambridge, MA: South End Press.

Massey, D.S., & Denton, N.A. (1993). *American apartheid: Segregation and the making of the underclass*. Cambridge, MA: Harvard University Press.

Mays, B.E. (1968). *The negro's God as reflected in his literature*. New York: Russell & Russell.

Mazama, A. (2003). *The Afrocentric paradigm*. Trenton, NJ: Africa World Press.

McNamee, S.J., & Miller, R.K., Jr. (2004). *The meritocracy myth*. Lanham, MD: Rowman & Littlefield.

McQuillar, T.L. (2007). *When rap music had a conscience: The artists, organizations and historic events that inspired and influenced the "Golden Age" of Hip- Hop from 1987 to 1996*. New York: Thunder's Mouth Press.

References

McWhorter, J.H. (2000). *Losing the race: Self-sabotage in black America*. New York: The Free Press.

MEE Productions. (1993). *Reaching the hip hop generation*. MEE Symposium: New York.

Micklethwait, J., & Wooldridge, A. (2004). *The right nation: Conservative power in America*. New York: Penguin Press.

Mills, C.W. (1997). *The racial contract*. Ithaca, NY: Cornell University Press.

Montagu, A. (1965). *The idea of race*. Lincoln: University of Nebraska.

Moynihan, D.P. (1970, March 3). Benign neglect for issue of race? *The Wall Street Journal*, p. 20.

Mukherjee, Roopali (2006). The ghetto fabulous aesthetic in contemporary black culture: Class and consumption in the barbershop films. *Cultural Studies, 20*(6), 599-629.

Murphy, J.W. & Choi, J.M. (1997). *Postmodernism, unraveling racism, and democratic institutions*. Westport, CT: Praeger.

Myers, L.J. (1991). Expanding the psychology of knowledge optimally: The importance of world view revisited. In R.L. Jones (Ed.), *Black Psychology* (3rd ed., pp. 15-28). Berkeley, CA: Cobb & Henry Publishers.

Myers, L.J. (1993). *Understanding an Afrocentric world view: Introduction to an optimal psychology* (2nd ed.). Dubuque, IA: Kendall/Hunt Publishing.

Myers, L.J. (1999). Theraputic processes for health and wholeness in the 21st century: Belief systems analysis and the paradigm shift. In R.L. Jones (Ed.), *Advances in African American Psychology* (pp. 313-355). Hampton, VA: Cobb & Henry Publishers.

Myrdal, G. (1944). *An American dilemma: The Negro problem and modern democracy* (vol. 1). New York: Harper & Row, Publishers.

Neubeck, K.J., & Cazenave, N.A. (2001). *Welfare racism: Playing the race card against America's poor*. New York: Routledge.

Neville, H.A., Coleman, M.N., Falconer, J.W., & Holmes, D. (2005). Color-blind racial ideology and psychological false consciousness among African Americans. *Journal of Black Psychology, 31*(1), 27-45.

Neville, H.A., Lilly, R.L., Duran, G., Lee, R., & Browne, L. (2000). Construction and initial validation of the Color-Blind Racial Scale (CoBRAS). *Journal of Counseling Pyschology, 47,* 59-70.

Neville, H.A., Worthington, R.L., & Spanierman, L.B. (2001). Race, power, and multicultural counseling psychology: Understanding White privilege and color-blind racial attitudes. In J.G. Ponterotto, J.M. Casas, L.A. Suzuki, & C.M. Alexander (Eds.), *Handbook of multicultural counseling* (2nd ed, pp. 257-288). Thousand Oaks, CA: Sage Publications.

Neville, R. (2003). *Amerika psycho: Behind Uncle Sam's mask of sanity.* New York: Ocean Press.

Newman, K.S. (1999). *No shame in my game: The working poor in the inner city.* New York: Alfred A. Knopf and The Russell Sage Foundation.

Nobles, W.W. (1980). African philosophy: Foundations for black psychology. In R.L. Jones (Ed.), *Black psychology* (pp. 18-32). New York: Harper & Row.

Nobles, W.W. (1991). African philosophy: Foundations for black psychology. In R.L. Jones (Ed.), *Black Psychology* (3rd ed., 47-63). Berkeley, CA: Cobb & Henry Publishers.

Nobles, W.W. (2006). *Seeking the Sakhu: Foundational writings for an African psychology.* Chicago: Third World Press.

Nobles, W.W., Lawford, L.G., Cavil, W.E., III (1985). *The KM EBIT HUSIA: Authoritative utterances of exceptional insight for the black family.* Oakland, CA: A Black Family Institute Publication.

Norris, C. (1990). *What's wrong with postmodernism: Critical theory and the ends of philosophy.* Baltimore: The John Hopkins University Press.

Obenga, T. (2002). Who am I? Interpretation in African historiography. In J.H. Carruthers & L.C. Harris (Eds.), *African world history project: The preliminary challenge* (pp. 31-44). Los Angeles: Association for the Study of Classical African Civilizations.

Omi, M. & Winant H. (1986). *Racial formation in the United States: From the 1960s to the 1980s.* New York: Routledge & Kegan Paul.

Omi, M., & Winant, H. (1994). *Racial formation in the United States from the 1960s to the 1990s* (2nd ed.). New York: Routledge.

References

Owens Smith, J. (1987). *The politics of racial inequality: A systematic comparative macro-analysis from the colonial period to 1970.* New York: Greenwood Press.

Outlaw, L.T., Jr. (1996). *On race and philosophy.* New York: Routledge.

Paris, P.J. (1995). *The spirituality of African peoples: The search for a common moral discourse.* Minneapolis: Fortress Press.

Patterson, O. (1997). *The ordeal of integration: Progress and resentment in America's "racial" crisis.* New York: Basic Civitas Books.

Payne, R.J. (1998). *Getting beyond race: The changing American culture.* Boulder, CO: Westview Press.

Pear, R., & Eckholm, E. (2006, August 21). A decade after welfare overhaul, a fundamental shift in policy and perception. *The New York Times*, pp. A12.

Philogene, G. (1999). *From Black to African American: A new social representation.* London: Praeger.

Pinn, A.B. (2002). *The black church in the post-Civil Rights era.* Maryknoll, NY: Orbis Books.

Piven, F.F. (2006). Why welfare is racist. In S.F. Schram, J. Soss, & R.C. Fording (Eds.), *Race and the politics of welfare reform* (pp. 323-335). Ann Arbor: University of Michigan Press.

Powell, J.A. (2007). Structural racism and spatial Jim Crow. In R. D. Bullard (Ed.), *The black metropolis in the twenty-first centruy: Race, power, and politics of race* (pp. 41-65). New York: Rowman & Littlefield.

Quigley, C. (1966). *Tragedy & Hope: A history of the world in our time.* New York: Macmillan.

Rajshekar, V.T. (1995). *Dalit: The black untouchables of India* (3rd ed.). Atlanta: Clarity Press.

Rangarajan, A., & Wood, R. (1999). *How WFNJ clients are faring under welfare reform: An early look.* Princeton, NJ: Mathematica Policy Research.

Rasor, S.C. & Dash, M.J.N. (2003). *The mark of Zion: Congregational life in Black churches.* Cleveland: The Pilgrim Press.

Rector, R. (2006, March 8). Renewing welfare reform. *The Washington Times*, p. A17.

Reed, I. (2003). *Another day at the front.* New York: Basic Books.

Reese, E. (2005). *Backlash against welfare mothers: Past + Present.* Berkeley: University of California Press.

Rose, T. (1994). *Black noise: Rap music and black culture in contemporary America.* London: Wesleyan University Press.

Rotunda, R.D. (1986). *The politics of language: Liberalism as word and symbol.* Iowa City: University of Iowa Press.

Ryan, W. (1971). *Blaming the victim.* New York: Pantheon Books.

Salins, P.D. (1997). *Assimilation, American style.* New York: Basic Books.

Schaefer, R.T. (2005). *Race and ethnicity in the United States* (3rd ed.). Upper Saddle River, NJ: Pearson Prentice Hall.

Schiller, H.I. (1973). *The mind managers.* Boston: Beacon Press.

Schlesinger, A.M., Jr. (1992). *The disuniting of America: Reflections on a multicultural society.* New York: W.W. Norton & Company.

Schram, S.F. (2006). Putting a black face on welfare: The good and the bad. In S.F. Schram, J. Soss, & R.C. Fording (Eds.), *Race and the politics of welfare reform* (pp. 196-221). Ann Arbor: The University of Michigan Press.

Sears, D.O., Hetts, J.J., Sidanius, J., & Bobo L. (2000). Race in American politics: Framing the debates. In D.O. Sears, J. Sidanius, & L. Bobo (Eds.), *Racialized politics: The debate about racism in America* (pp. 1-43). Chicago: The University of Chicago Press.

Semmes, C.E. (1992). *Cultural hegemony and African American development.* Westport, CT: Praeger.

Senate Republican Policy Committee. (2007). *Fair minimum wage act of 2007.* (H.R. 2, Calendar No. 5). Washington, DC.

Sidanius, J., & Pratto, F. (1999). *Social dominance: An intergroup theory of social hierarchy and oppression.* New York: Cambridge University Press.

Skinner, B.F. (1969). *Contingencies of reinforcement: A theoretical analysis.* New York: Appleton-Century-Crofts.

Skinner, E.P. (1999). The restoration of African identity for a new millennium. In I. Okpewho, C. Boyce Davies, & A.A. Mazrui (Eds.), *The African diaspora: African origins and New World identities* (pp. 28-45). Bloomington: Indiana University Press.

References

Smith, P. (1988). *Discerning the subject*. Minneapolis: University of Minnesota Press.

Smith, R.C. (1995). *Racism in the post-Civil Rights era*. Albany: State University of New York Press.

Smith, R.L., Jr. (2007). *From strength to strength: Shaping a black practical theology for the 21st century*. New York: Peter Lang.

Soss, J., Schram, S., Vartanian, T., & O'Brien, E. (2001). Setting the terms of relief: Explaining state policy choices in the devolution revolution. *American Journal of Political Science, 45*(2), 378-396.

Sowell, T. (2005). *Black rednecks and white liberals*. San Francisco: Encounter Books.

Steele, S. (1990). *The content of our character: A new vision of race in America*. New York: St. Martin's Press.

Steinberg, S. (1995). *Turning back: The retreat from racial justice in American thought and policy*. Boston: Beacon Press.

Sumner, W.G. (1925). *What social classes owe each other*. New Haven, CT: Yale University Press.

Sutherland, M. (1997). *Black authenticity: A psychology for liberating people of African descent*. Chicago: Third World Press.

Swan, L.A. (1981). *Survival and progress: The Afro-American experience*. Westport, CT: Greenwood Press.

Sykes, C.J. (1992). *A nation of victims: The decay of the American character*. New York: St. Martin's Press.

Terkel, S. (1992). *Race: How blacks and whites think and feel about the American obsession*. New York: The New Press.

Tomlinson, J. (1991). *Cultural imperialism: a critical introduction*. Baltimore: The John Hopkins University Press.

Van Horne, W.A. (1997). Introduction. In W.A. Van Horne (Ed.), *Global convulsions: Race, ethnicity, and nationalism at the end of the twentieth century* (pp. 1-45). Albany: State University of New York Press.

Wacquant, L. (2006). From slavery to mass incarceration: Rethinking the "race Question" in the United States. In Macedo, D. & Gounari, P. (Eds.), *The globalization of racism* (pp. 94-110). Boulder, CO: Paradigm Publishers.

Walters, R.W. (2003). *White nationalism Black interests: Conservative public policy and the Black community.* Detroit: Wayne State University Press.

Washington, J.R., Jr. (1978). Introduction . In Washington, J.R., Jr. (Ed.), *Black religion and public policy: Ethical and historical perspectives* (pp. i-vi). [S.I. : s.n.], 1978 .

Watkins, S.C. (1998). *Representing: Hip hop culture and the production of black cinema.* Chicago: The University of Chicago Press.

Watts, L.W. (1974). Caucuses and caucasians. In C.E. Lincoln (Ed.), *The black experience in religion* (pp. 24-28). Garden City, NY: Anchor Press/Doubleday.

Welsing, F.C. (1991). *The Isis papers: The keys to the colors.* Washington, DC: CW Publishing.

West, C. (1992). Nihilism in Black America. In G. Dent (Ed.), *Black popular culture* (pp. 37-47). Seattle: Bay Press.

West, C. (1993). *Race matters.* Boston: Beacon Press.

West, C. (1999). *The Cornel West reader.* New York: Basic Civitas Books.

White, J.L. & Parham, T.A. (1990). *The psychology of blacks: An African-American perspective* (2nd ed.). Englewood Cliffs, NJ: Prentice Hall.

Will, G.F. (2006, June 5). White guilt, deciphered. *Newsweek, 68.*

Williams, A. (1995). *Beyond blame: How we can succeed by breaking the dependency barrier.* New York: Free Press.

Williams, J. (2006). *Enough: The phony leaders, dead-end movement, and culture of failure that are undermining Black America – and what we can do about it.* New York: Crown Publishers.

Williams, R.L. (1972). Abuses and misuses in testing black children. In R.L. Jones (Ed.), *Black psychology* (pp. 77-91). New York: Harper & Row, Publishers.

Williams, W.E. (1987). *All it takes is guts: A minority view.* Washington, DC: Regnery Books.

Williams Crenshaw, K. (1988). Race, reform, and retrenchment: Trasformation and legitimation in antidiscrimination law. *Harvard Law Review, 101*(7), 1131- 1387.

References

Wilmore, G.S. (1983). *Black religion and black radicalism: An interpretation of the religious history of Afro-American people* (2nd ed.). New York: Orbis Books.

Wilson, A.N. (1992). *Understanding black adolescent male violence: Its prevention and remediation.* New York: Afrikan World InfoSystems.

Wilson, A.N. (1993). *The falsification of Afrikan consciousness: Eurocentric history, psychiatry and the politics of white supremacy.* New York: Afrikan World InfoSystems.

Wilson, A.N. (1998). *Blueprint for black power: A moral, political and economic imperative for the twenty-first century.* New York: Afrikan World InfoSystems.

Wilson, A.N. (1999). *Afrikan-centered consciousness versus the new world order: Garveyism in the age of globalism.* New York: Afrikan World InfoSystems.

Wilson, A.N. (2005). *Blueprint for black power: A moral, political and economic imperative for the twenty-first century.* New York: Afrikan World InfoSystems.

Wilson, B.M. (2000). *Race and Place in Birmingham: The Civil Rights and neighborhood movements.* Lanham, MD: Rowman and Littlefield Publishers.

Wilson, D. (2007). *Cities and race: America's new black ghetto.* London: Routledge Taylor & Francis Group.

Wilson, W.J. (1973). *Power, racism, and privilege: Race relations in theoretical and sociohistorical perspectives.* New York: The Free Press.

Wilson, W.J. (1987). *The truly disadvantaged: The inner city, the underclass, and public policy.* Chicago: The University of Chicago Press.

Wilson, W.J. (1996). *When work disappears: The world of the new urban poor.* New York: Vintage Books.

Wimberly, E.P., & Wimberly, A.S. (1986). *Liberation & human wholeness: The conversion experiences of Black people in slavery and freedom.* Nashville, TN: Abingdon.

Winant, H. (1994). *Racial Conditions: Politics, theory, comparisons.* Minneapolis: University of Minnesota Press.

Winant, H. (2001). *The world is a ghetto: Race and democracy since World War II.* New York: Basic Books.

Winant, H. (2004). *The new politics of race: Globalism, difference, justice.* Minneapolis: University of Minnesota Press.

Woodson, C.G. (1922). *The Negro in our history.* Washington, DC: The Associated Publishers.

Woodson, C.G. (2000). *The Miseducation of the Negro* (1st ed.). Chicago: African American Images.

Wortham, A. (1981). *The other side of racism: A philosophic study of black race consciousness.* Columbus: Ohio State University Press.

Wright, B.E. (1984). *The psychopathic racial personality and other essays.* Chicago: Third World Press.

Wright Edelman, M. (1995, November 3). Say no to this welfare reform [Letter to The Editor]. *The Washington Post*, pp. A23.

Wright, W.D. (1998). *Racism matters.* Westport, CT: Praeger.

Wright, W.D. (2007). *Crisis of the black intellectual.* Chicago: Third World Press.

Young, J. & Braziel, J.E. (2006). Cultural amnesia and the Academy: Why the problem of the twenty-first century is still the "problem of the color line." In J. Young & J.E. Braziel (Eds.), *Race and the foundations of knowledge: Cultural amnesia in the Academy* (pp. 1-31). Urbana: University of Illinois Press.

Young, R. (2006). Putting materialism back into race theory: Toward a transformative theory of race. In J. Young & J.E. Braziel (Eds.), *Race and the foundations of knowledge: Cultural amnesia in the Academy* (pp. 32- 45). Urbana: University of Illinois Press.

Zizek, S. (1997). Multiculturalism, or, the cultural logic of multinational capitalism. *New Left Review, 225,* 28-29.

Index